Joe Galante

D1454728

PLANNING
CLASSROOM
MANAGEMENT

SECOND EDITION

PLANNING CLASSROOM MANAGEMENT

A Five-Step Process to Creating a Positive Learning Environment

SECOND EDITION

Karen Bosch

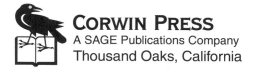

CORWIN PRESS
A SAGE Publications Company
Thousand Oaks, California

Copyright © 2006 by Corwin Press

All rights reserved. When forms and sample documents are included, their use is authorized only by educators, local school sites, and/or noncommercial or nonprofit entities who have purchased the book. Except for that usage, no part of this book may be reproduced or utilized in any form or by any means, electronic or mechanical, including photocopying, recording, or by any information storage and retrieval system, without permission in writing from the publisher.

For information:

Corwin Press
A Sage Publications Company
2455 Teller Road
Thousand Oaks, California 91320
www.corwinpress.com

Sage Publications Ltd.
1 Oliver's Yard
55 City Road
London EC1Y 1SP
United Kingdom

Sage Publications India Pvt. Ltd.
B-42, Panchsheel Enclave
Post Box 4109
New Delhi 110 017 India

Printed in the United States of America.

This book is printed on acid-free paper.

Library of Congress Cataloging-in-Publication Data

Bosch, Karen
Planning classroom management: A five-step process to creating a positive learning environment / Karen Bosch.— 2nd ed.
    p. cm.
Includes bibliographical references and index.
ISBN 978-1-4129-3767-2 (cloth) — ISBN 978-1-4129-3768-9 (pbk.)
    1. Classroom management—Planning. I. Title.

LB3013.B62 2006
371.102′4—dc22   2006001771

09   10   10   9   8   7   6   5   4   3   2

Acquisitions Editor:	Cathy Hernandez
Editorial Assistant:	Charline Wu
Project Editor:	Kate Peterson
Copy Editor:	Teresa Herlinger
Typesetter:	C&M Digitals (P) Ltd.
Indexer:	Kay Dusheck
Cover Designer:	Scott Van Atta

Contents

Preface

Over the past 10 years, I have initiated many discussions with teachers and asked them to describe classroom management. Although the term is widely used in education, the teachers I spoke with found the concept of classroom management difficult to verbalize, much less define. The following are some of their responses:

"I guess it is that difference in some classrooms."

"It is a hope, dream, and a wish."

"All teachers want it. It is something that some teachers have and others do not. It is something I wish I had."

"It is magic!"

"It is what you need to be successful."

"If you are having trouble, you better get management."

"It is like law and order!"

"I read about it but I still don't know if I have it."

"You are lucky if you have it!"

Many books and articles are available to help teachers create a well-managed classroom. However, *Planning Classroom Management: A Five-Step Process to Creating a Positive Learning Environment* is unlike others because it offers the reader more than a definition of the term and a presentation of theorists and their ideas on classroom management. *Planning Classroom Management* provides a model for classroom management by demonstrating it as a process. By following the steps in the process, teachers learn to observe and identify how classroom management works and then develop and implement a personal classroom management plan (CMP) in their classrooms.

The contents of this book have been field-tested for more than 10 years by preservice teachers in undergraduate and graduate programs and students in alternative certification programs (shorter, condensed programs). Preservice teachers agreed that the classroom management Observation Guide kept them focused and on task when they conducted classroom observations. One alternative program student said, "The Observation Guide served as an integrative activity that put all the content I was learning into a format that I could take directly to the classroom."

The book, the Observation Guide, and the classroom management plan (CMP) have been reviewed by more than 100 practicing teachers for suggestions, clarifications, and feedback. Administrators and principals reviewed the material, provided their perspective on classroom management, and described their expectations for how teachers and classrooms should work. One school administrator commented that this text finally makes classroom management approachable and available for all teachers. A principal stated he is thrilled that someone has attempted to demystify this term and give all educators a chance to really know what classroom management is and how to pursue it. Discussion with the school administrators revealed that adopting and mandating a districtwide or even schoolwide discipline approach has never worked because it soon became random, inconsistent, and arbitrary at the classroom level. They concluded that this book and its approach integrate concepts of teacher personality, management, and instruction as well as current thoughts on discipline and articulate them into a plan that can be successful in every classroom.

Several school personnel recruiters in Virginia thought it impressive that preservice teachers' portfolios included a personal classroom management plan. Upon hiring one of the graduates who participated in the CMP field test, one superintendent of schools in Tennessee said that based on the CMP, he felt he was hiring an experienced teacher.

ORGANIZATION OF THE BOOK

Planning Classroom Management A Five-Step Process to Creating a Positive Learning Environment describes the development of a personal classroom management plan. Questions, activities, and examples throughout the text help teachers further explore and understand classroom management as a process. Descriptions of how teachers can use a CMP appear in each chapter. Some of these examples are fictional; others are based on actual teacher accounts of the value of the CMP in their classrooms.

Specifically, Chapter 1, Classroom Management, provides an overview of classroom management and how to use the book. This chapter outlines the five steps of the classroom management process—introspection, classroom observation, development of the CMP, implementation of the CMP, and revision of the CMP—and the importance of a classroom management plan.

Chapter 2, Classroom Management Plan, describes the CMP and outlines the four components of the CMP: classroom organization, instruction, evaluation, and professional development.

Chapter 3, Introspection: Getting in Touch With Your Teaching Self, describes the first step in the process of creating a CMP. The classroom management process begins with introspection. The questions and activities in Chapter 3 are designed to assist the teacher in identifying his or her teaching self. Teacher reflection also includes the thought processes teachers engage in outside the classroom. Getting in touch with their thoughts, attitudes, and personality styles, both inside and outside the classroom, allows teachers to focus the CMP to capitalize on personal strong areas and strengthen weak areas. Having identified thought processes and other internal characteristics, the next step is for teachers to step outside themselves and observe teaching practices and behaviors of practicing teachers.

The Observation Guide in Chapter 4, Classroom Observation, helps teachers observe and record specific classroom information, which they then use to develop their CMP. The See, Hear, and Feel method helps teachers record the classroom setting and operation. Other sections help teachers collect information on classroom management in operation—what it is, how it works, when it works, and why it works. Teachers are encouraged to visit many classrooms and interview many teachers using the Observation Guide.

In Chapter 5, Developing a Personal Classroom Management Plan, the teacher composes his or her own CMP. The information gathered in Chapters 3 and 4 serves as a resource in developing the personal CMP.

Chapter 6, Implementing the Classroom Management Plan, focuses on how to teach the CMP to the class—the implementation step of the process. In addition to guidance on planning and writing lessons to teach the CMP, this section offers CMP mini-lessons that teachers can incorporate into the curriculum.

Chapter 7, Revising the Classroom Management Plan, focuses on reflective thinking and offers a method that turns reflection into revision and thinking into action. A teacher's personal CMP remains a dynamic, ever-changing script for effective classroom management.

Chapter 8, Samples of Effective Teachers' Classroom Management Plans, offers five sample CMPs written by teachers of primary, intermediate, middle, and secondary grades to give further guidance on creating an effective CMP.

The second edition of this text has been modified and enhanced by feedback received from professors and students using the first edition in teacher preparation courses and field experiences, beginning teachers using the CMP in their first year, and mentors reflecting on ways to help mentees improve their classroom management. Several enhancements have been made to provide an even clearer understanding of the development of the personal classroom management plan.

This edition expands on the descriptions of the CMP components— classroom organization, instruction, evaluation, and professional development—and includes a greater number of references to the research that underpins the text's critical concepts. More attention has been given to managing the diverse student populations found in classrooms, so that the CMP is practical, relevant, and effective in structuring successful classroom management for all learners. In addition, more emphasis has been placed on reflective teaching practices for professional growth and development and on the importance of reflective revising of the CMP.

USING THIS BOOK

Planning Classroom Management: A Five-Step Process to Creating a Positive Learning Environment meets an important need for both preservice and practicing teachers. The term *preservice teacher* refers to a student enrolled in a teacher education program and involved with field experiences, from the initial levels of classroom observation to the student teaching experience. A *practicing teacher* currently teaches in a classroom. The classroom management process is easy to teach, learn, and implement. It can be done by everyone involved with classroom teaching. It can be done individually, by teams, by grade levels, or as a schoolwide effort. It can be taught to any number of teachers at one time or any combination of teachers. For example, it could be an inservice activity for a school, all sixth-grade teachers, all math teachers, all first-year teachers, all teachers needing remediation, and so on. For remediation purposes, principals and teachers must often devise a self-improvement plan. The process described in this book provides a direct, responsive, nonthreatening plan for improvement.

Planning Classroom Management is aimed primarily at preservice and practicing teachers, although others involved in education will also find the information extremely useful. Undergraduate and graduate teacher education students could use it as a primary text in methods courses in education, when doing observations, in practicums, and in the student teaching experience. Teacher education programs can require preservice teachers to make observations throughout the program and may require the development of a personal CMP for use in the first year of teaching.

The CMP could be included in a comprehensive teacher's portfolio and in a mini-portfolio used when interviewing for school positions and left with the principal. This mini-portfolio may include a resume, a teaching philosophy statement, a CMP, scores from required tests, letters of recommendation, and evaluations from field experiences. The CMP, portfolio, and mini-portfolio are valuable assets in securing a teaching position.

The description of the classroom management process is particularly helpful to the alternative certification student. The alternative certification program—usually a shorter, condensed teacher preparation program—is for people who are changing careers and many of them have little classroom experience. This text highlights the most important information in organizing a classroom and structuring teacher and student autonomy. An alternative certification student writes, "My CMP has become my learning rubric. I am beginning to understand how we learn, what can impede us in the learning process, what strategies will work for me, and how to structure those strategies into a personal CMP."

Facing their first teaching job, many new teachers worry about what to do first. Beginning, maintaining, and ending the year with a management plan can alleviate some of this apprehension. In addition, this book provides an opportunity for both preservice and practicing teachers to prepare before the first year of teaching or the school year begins.

Many practicing teachers who may feel burned out or ready to give up or who want more from teaching would benefit from constructing or reconstructing a plan for classroom management. Teachers returning to the profession can prepare a CMP before entering the classroom. Teachers changing grade levels can construct a CMP appropriate to that grade level before the year begins. Teachers moving from school to school, area to area, or state to state can take the CMP with them.

Principals, school administrators, district supervisors, and superintendents can endorse this classroom management process because it offers consistency, efficiency, and effectiveness in setting standards of classroom operation. It is easy to implement as a schoolwide and districtwide policy. Knowing what to do and how to do it, faculty and staff can assist and support each other. A team of teachers can develop a CMP together by grade level or subject area.

This book can support teacher induction programs. The classroom management process developed in this book gets to the heart of the concerns and problems of teachers searching for classroom management. The book can help both mentor and mentee establish a cooperative dialogue in communicating essentials of teaching, collecting and sharing information, developing a CMP, and reflecting on specific information for professional growth and development.

THE IMPORTANCE OF A CLASSROOM MANAGEMENT PLAN

Public education is important to nearly all Americans, and the public's concerns are high on the national agenda. According to the 36th Annual Phi Delta Kappa/Gallup Poll of the Public's Attitudes Toward the Public Schools (Rose & Gallup, 2005), 47 percent of respondents awarded the nation's public schools a grade of A or B, and 61 percent of respondents rated their local public schools a grade of A or B. Topping the list of public concerns was the lack of financial support (21%) with lack of discipline and overcrowded schools tied for second place (10%). Discipline dominated the poll as a major concern until 2000. In 2001, the lack of financial support tied for first place with the concern for discipline. However, since 2001, lack of financial support has claimed the top spot. Discipline, overcrowded schools, use of drugs, and fighting/violence/gangs consistently remain on the list as public concerns (Rose & Gallup, 2005). In *Education 97/98*, Elam, Rose, and Gallup (1997a) state the following:

> One of the principal goals of education is to produce individuals capable of clear moral judgment and self-control. But in the real school world, establishing a climate for the development of self-control as well as for academic achievement often requires the exercise of external authority and control. (p. 33)

Educators know that, ultimately, exercising external authority and control is not the answer. The answer lies within people. Self-control is an educational goal that needs to be developed in schools. *Planning Classroom Management: A Five-Step Process to Creating a Positive Learning Environment* contains a format that assists a beginning or practicing teacher, a teacher new to a school system, a teacher new to a grade level, and even a teacher seeking remediation. The hope is that the text challenges school administrators, teachers, and teacher educators to rethink the rhetoric of classroom management. It adds promise to teacher preparation programs and for teachers seeking to improve their teaching by making classroom management a process and, therefore, accessible to every teacher and every classroom. *Planning Classroom Management: A Five-Step Process to Creating a Positive Learning Environment* can place teachers and students in a position to meet the demands for higher standards, more discipline in the classrooms, and improved student learning.

The time has come to replace, if not eliminate, the words guess, hope, dream, wish, magic, and luck from teachers' discussion of classroom management. The time has come to take the term classroom management and make it a process that can be taught, learned, and implemented in today's classrooms.

Acknowledgments

A very special acknowledgment goes to my husband, Gordon, and daughter, Morghan. Their support of my writing projects allows me to remain in front of the computer many days from dawn to late into the evening hours.

I want to thank the many preservice and practicing teachers who field-tested the Observation Guide, wrote classroom management lesson plans, and shared their own classroom management plans in this book. Special recognition goes to the following people for their much appreciated efforts: Kimberly Hammers, Lynn Seltzer, Heide McCleery, Brittany Voyles, Les Allen Fortune, Lindsay Crump Porzio, D. L. Achterfeld, Shreve Cassarino, Susan G. Smith, Rebecca Barrett, Debra-Ann F. Brooks, Melanie A. Burnor, Sonya L. Huss, John C. Sammons, Linda M. Sherbinsky, Elizabeth T. Gardner, Holly L. Smith, Kimberly V. Ritter, and "K" Stone.

PUBLISHER'S ACKNOWLEDGMENTS

Corwin Press gratefully acknowledges the contributions of the following reviewers:

O. Gilbert Brown, Associate Dean of Students
Adjunct Associate Professor, Higher Education
Indiana University-Bloomington, Bloomington, IN

Frances Fowler, Professor of Educational Leadership
Director of Graduate Studies, Department of Educational Leadership
Miami University, Oxford, OH

Francisco Guajardo, Assistant Professor of Educational Leadership,
   Department of Educational Leadership
University of Texas Pan American, Edinburg, TX

Mary Johnstone, Principal
Rabbit Creek Elementary School, Anchorage, AK

Arlene C. Miguel, Principal
Hampden Meadows School, Barrington, RI

About the Author

 Karen Bosch, PhD, is a professor of education and Director of Teacher Education at Virginia Wesleyan College in Norfolk, Virginia. She has been awarded the Most Inspiring Faculty Award from Old Dominion University and most recently has become the recipient of the Virginia Wesleyan College's Batten Distinguished Faculty Award for excellence in teaching, scholarship, and passion for inspiring others. Along with the previous edition of this volume, Karen has also written the book *The First-Year Teacher*, which prepares and supports beginning teachers in their first year and beyond. She has published articles in *Middle School Journal, Current Issues in Middle Level Education, Clearing House, Journal of Computing in Education*, and *Journal of Research on Computing in Education.* As an educational consultant, she conducts seminars and workshops on classroom management and effective teaching practices. She has presented her research and her teacher preparation program models at conferences nationwide. She was formerly a public school teacher and administrator.

1

Classroom Management

Fourth-grade teacher Steve Ames is about to conduct a science lesson on earthquakes. Having just placed their chairs in a semicircle in the center of the room, his students are not yet settled as they chat with their neighbors, their reading books closed in their laps. Steve places his chair in the center of the students and as he sits, he raises one finger. In seconds the students are silent, turning in their seats to face him. Steve raises a second finger, and the students open their books to the assigned pages. He asks the students to describe an earthquake. Several students raise their hands and Steve calls on each, listening intently and nodding approvingly as they each give their definition of an earthquake. When one student responds to another of Steve's questions without raising his hand, another student quietly reminds the outspoken student to wait his turn.

Is this scene merely a teacher's dream? No. It is a description of a typical lesson in Steve Ames's classroom. How does he do it? Steve Ames has a classroom management plan.

His classes were not always so organized. It once took too much time to get students to come to order, to pay attention. Too often, they were distracted by the antics of their fellow students or they wrote each other notes instead of doing their class work. When they did pay attention, they were reluctant to contribute to class discussions. But now the students are attentive and engaged in the lesson; often they work in teams to teach each other the lesson. They don't have time to get into trouble. They have accepted responsibility for the classroom environment, and they are not about to break the rules Steve asked them to create.

OVERVIEW OF CLASSROOM MANAGEMENT

Nearly every teacher agrees that classroom management is an important aspect of successful teaching. Fewer agree on how to achieve it, and even fewer claim the concept of classroom management is operating in their own classrooms.

Classroom management and discipline, terms often used interchangeably, are not synonymous. Teachers asked to define classroom management in one word have given the following responses: discipline, control, and consequences. Discipline was always the first word they chose. In the last few years, however, teachers have responded with the following words: organization, control, positive climate, and incentives. In effect, discipline has become a much smaller part of the term classroom management. Classroom management is much more than any one of these words or the sum of all these words (Charles, 1992; Wolfgang, 1995).

Classroom management means how the teacher works, how the class works, how the teacher and students work together, and how teaching and learning happen. For students, classroom management means having some control in how the class operates and understanding clearly the way the teacher and students are to interact with each other. For both teachers and students, classroom management is not a condition but a process.

Classroom Management: Gift or Skill?

Many teachers, especially beginning teachers, cite classroom management as an ever-present concern (Rogers & Freiberg, 1994; Veenman, 1984). A meta-analysis of the past 50 years of classroom research identified classroom management as the most important factor, even above student aptitude, affecting student learning (Wang, Haertel, & Walberg, 1994). But contrary to popular belief, classroom management is not a gift bestowed upon some teachers. While it's true that some teachers adapt to classroom management techniques easily, making it look to their colleagues like they possess some innate talent, classroom management is a skill—a skill that can be taught like any other, and, most importantly, a skill that like any other must be practiced to achieve proficiency.

Although much has been written about classroom management, teachers have not been taught comprehensive, practical methods of improving classroom management, and little emphasis has been placed on "helping teachers understand the issues in effective classroom management and the relationship among various strategies" (Jones & Jones, 2004, p. 1).

Many teachers try classroom management ideas and strategies, tossing them spontaneously and inconsistently into the classroom, then become discouraged when the classroom they hope for does not materialize. Effective classroom management does require specific skills such as planning, organizing, and reflecting as well as an aptitude for teamwork and perseverance. It requires a great deal of commitment initially, then a willingness to adjust one's thinking and actions as one learns what works and what does not work.

But teachers cannot implement a definition. When teachers see that classroom management is a process—a process they can follow, learn, and implement in their own classrooms—they understand that they can tailor the process to match their specific skills and needs. In other words, they can set themselves up for success, not failure. In addition, they recognize that the process is ongoing. Just as teachers change with experience and attempt to meet the changing needs of their students, so their classroom management plan must adapt as well.

CREATING A CLASSROOM MANAGEMENT PLAN

A classroom management plan (CMP) is not only a means of organizing a classroom. The plan gives structure to everything that goes on in the classroom—from the seating arrangement to the lessons to the grading of homework assignments to the relationships among classmates. As an antenna eliminates static, improving television reception, so a CMP eliminates distractions and allows teachers to focus on teaching and students to focus on learning. Because teachers and students alike know exactly what to expect in the classroom, the plan fosters a sense of community, of everyone working toward the same goal.

There is no magic formula for creating a CMP. In fact, while all teachers may have similar components in their CMPs, no two plans will be the same. That is because to be effective, a CMP must reflect a teacher's personality and teaching style. It will work precisely because the teacher feels comfortable with it. The purpose of this book, *Planning Classroom Management,* is to guide teachers in the preparation of a CMP. The text takes teachers through the process of creating a personal CMP, a process that has proved effective with preservice and practicing teachers.

The Classroom Management Process

The five steps of the classroom management process are covered in Chapters 3 through 7. The classroom management process is as follows: introspection (Chapter 3), classroom observation (Chapter 4), development of the CMP (Chapter 5), implementation of the CMP (Chapter 6), and revision of the CMP (Chapter 7).

In brief, the first step, introspection, asks teachers to identify and bridge the gap between their personal self and their teaching self. The second step, classroom observation, requires observing other teachers and being able to identify specific management structures and strategies that make a class work. The third step is the initial development of the CMP. The fourth step, implementation of the plan in the classroom, prepares teachers to teach the CMP. The final step has teachers revise the plan for more classroom management effectiveness. The steps are shown in Figure 1.1.

It's important to note that teachers could simply fill out the CMP template (see Figure 5.1 in Chapter 5) and believe they have a plan for classroom

Figure 1.1

> **Classroom Management Process**
>
> 1. Introspection
>
> 2. Observation
>
> 3. Development of the classroom management plan (CMP)
>
> 4. Implementation of the CMP
>
> 5. Revision of the CMP

management. But it is the *process* that helps teachers improve their classroom management skills, not the answers to the CMP questions. For through the process, teachers internalize the responses. Through the process, teachers face their strengths and weaknesses as educators, learn to evaluate objectively their teaching effectiveness, and, perhaps most importantly, come to understand that as they grow and change, so must the CMP. The very act of completing the process makes a teacher a better teacher.

2

Classroom Management Plan

First-year teacher Kathryn Flaherty was ecstatic when she was offered the position teaching third grade at Meadowlark Elementary School. She spent the weeks before school started decorating her classroom with colorful posters and artwork, rearranging the desks into perfect rows, making sure she had plenty of supplies, from whiteboard markers to blank transparencies for the overhead. A stickler for details, she had the first three weeks of lessons worked out and written neatly in her lesson planner. She knew the subjects she would cover forward and backward and felt she was prepared for any questions the students might have.

On the first day of class, she greeted her students enthusiastically and started right in on her first lesson. But her carefully made lesson plans did not tell her what to do when the students didn't pay attention day after day. They didn't help her cope with one particularly ill-behaved student whose antics, while not destructive or harmful, were a constant distraction to the other students. They didn't tell her how to get students to respond to her excellent open-ended questions. When she placed the students in pairs or groups of three to work, they, and she, accomplished even less. When a friend phoned her to inquire about her first weeks on the job, Kathryn said simply, "I was doing just fine until the kids showed up."

Clearly, Kathryn didn't have a classroom management plan (CMP). A teacher with a CMP will not look or feel like a beginner. With the support of the CMP, a teacher sends a message not only to students but to administrators and parents that she knows what she is doing.

WHAT IS A CLASSROOM MANAGEMENT PLAN?

Les Fortune, a Virginia Beach, Virginia, Teacher of the Year, writes,

> Classroom management is the most misunderstood term in the educator's vocabulary. All teachers seek it, parents expect it, and administrators demand it. Should an administrator enter the classroom for an observation, the teacher is most cognizant that his or her performance will be judged primarily on the merits of viewed classroom management—not learning, a far more difficult accomplishment to measure.

The quote above underscores the conundrum that is classroom management—it's tough to define but everyone knows when it's not there. This teacher effectively characterizes both the significant and the intangible nature of classroom management. But classroom management need not be so elusive. The purpose of the classroom management plan is to put, literally and figuratively, the tools for classroom management in teachers' hands.

In a nutshell, a CMP structures teaching, student learning, and autonomy and provides a sense of community in a classroom. But the best way to describe and define a CMP is to discuss each of its components and their effect on classroom management. The four primary components of the CMP are classroom organization, instruction, evaluation, and professional development (see Figure 2.1).

Figure 2.1

> **Four Components of a Classroom Management Plan**
>
> 1. Classroom Organization—the classroom environment and the classroom operation
>
> 2. Instruction—Lessons and effective teaching practices
>
> 3. Evaluation—Grading scheme and procedures
>
> 4. Professional Development—Reflection and additional training/education

THE COMPONENTS OF A CLASSROOM MANAGEMENT PLAN

Creating an effective CMP that incorporates the four components, from classroom organization and instruction to evaluation and professional development, can be done by following the five-step classroom management process (see Chapters 3–7). Teachers with a CMP have more than a "plan on paper": completing the process provides their classrooms with structure and creates a sense of community in a classroom.

Classroom Organization

The first component of the classroom management plan is how the classroom is organized to support teacher instruction and student learning. It encompasses the classroom environment (the physical aspects such as lighting, temperature, decorations, and the setup, comfort, and proximity of furniture) and the classroom operation (aspects the teacher imposes such as rules, routines, consequences, and incentives). According to Emmer, Evertson, Clements, and Worsham (1997), effective room layout will be guided by attention to three elements—visibility, accessibility, and lack of distractibility.

Classroom environment

The physical environment should make students enjoy coming to class. The room should be bright and welcoming, with student work displayed on the walls and bulletin boards. Most important, students should feel safe there.

The placement of desks must allow students to view the chalkboard and the screen used with the overhead projector and allow the teacher to access the desks easily (Simmons, 2002). Enz (1997) explains that good room arrangement involves much thought and planning, far beyond the physical placement of desks. It is important that students can see the teacher, chalkboard, and media projections and the teacher can observe each student as well as scan the whole class. Simmons concludes that consideration should be given to desk arrangement for ease and efficiency of movement by students when working in groups. The classroom should have traffic patterns carefully established for frequent activities such as to reach the pencil sharpener, go to the board, and exit the room.

The environment makes it easier or more difficult to implement classroom management. For example, the seating arrangement can support or discourage the aim of a lesson. Straight rows with the teacher's desk in front may be neat and orderly, but this arrangement contributes little to a sense of classroom community. Desks arranged in a semi-circle or groups of four promote discussion and working and learning together. The teacher's desk in the back of the room instead of the front signals that the students are the most important part of the class. Students' work displayed on the bulletin boards, interactive bulletin boards for instruction and improved learning, and student-designed bulletin boards not only enhance the environment but also give students a role in planning that environment. Researchers Emmer, Evertson, and Worsham (2003) have concluded that how the room is arranged and how the rules and procedures are emphasized are important in getting the school year off to a good start.

Classroom operation

The other aspect of classroom organization is the formulated policies, rules, incentives, consequences, established routines, and procedures that fall under the heading of classroom operation. Perhaps the most important item under classroom operation is rules.

Whether the teacher refers to them as rules, rights, expectations, or responsibilities, these principles govern classroom operation and become the written and unwritten code that allows a classroom to work. The classroom is set up as a democracy, with teacher and students working together to create and enforce the rules and establish guidelines for behavior. The rules created by the teacher and students support a task-oriented learning community in which teacher and students share expectations. Once they have a role in making the classroom work, students become more accountable for *how* it works. All students must understand the rules, and everyone must know the consequences for not following rules.

Consequences are a part of every classroom. Teachers should solicit student input in establishing consequences as well as rules. Students then choose their behavior with full understanding of the consequences, and, one hopes, they will choose discipline and self-control. The use of rules and consequences students help create teaches them that they are accountable for their actions and, as a result, builds students' feelings of self-reliance and self-respect.

Routines and procedures are a vital part of efficient classroom operation. Routines help with everyday administrative tasks such as taking attendance and recording lunch options. Other examples of daily routines include the teacher greeting students at the door every morning, the pledge of allegiance, and the recitation of the class motto as well as journal writing, copying objectives from the chalkboard, responding to a verbal or math challenge, reading aloud to students after lunch, and a 10-minute pack down just before school ends. Procedures might cover the proper time and way to request use of the bathroom pass and the pencil sharpener, to turn in homework and in-class assignments, or to seek teacher assistance.

Teachers send messages, spoken and unspoken, to students all day long. Students send such messages as well. These messages are commonly referred to as cues. Cues are the nonverbal and verbal signs, signals, gestures, and body language teachers and students use to communicate with each other without using the standard way of speaking. Teachers can use this form of communication to send specific messages and expectations quickly and efficiently. For example, to begin a lesson, a teacher's cue might be raising his hand and moving to the center of the room. Another teacher might raise her index finger to her lips, a cue requesting silence. Students enjoy learning cues and assuming responsibility for responding to the cues appropriately without the teacher speaking a word.

Many teachers include incentives in their classroom operation. Teachers need to think carefully about incentives and decide the role they wish incentives to play in their classroom. If offered, incentives must be relevant, age appropriate, inviting, fun, desired, and readily chosen over the consequences. Incentives can create and sustain effort, persistence, enthusiasm, satisfaction, and empowerment.

The terms *incentives* and *rewards* are often used interchangeably in education literature; however, incentives are much more than rewards. Incentives are a way to help a student choose to work toward a goal, while reward suggests the behavior may not be inherently worthwhile but requires a prize to accomplish. Using the term incentive implies acceptance of some responsibility and a focus on learning rather than a focus on the reward. Even more simply, rewards are thought of as receiving something, whereas incentives are accomplishing something. Incentives can help promote goals, reinforce learning, maintain effort, enhance achievement, create enthusiasm, alter attitudes, promote self-control, strengthen appropriate behaviors, and achieve desired behaviors. Most important, incentives are fun, user-friendly, risk-free, and inexpensive motivators. Incentives provide teachers with a powerful alternative to discipline, reprimands, threats, yelling, and telling. Often incentives provide the classroom with a sense of community, camaraderie, and satisfaction as students work together to accomplish the goals of the incentives (see Figure 2.2).

Incentives can be the catalyst for students to improve their behavior, increase their academic involvement, strive for progress, and achieve success. Their effects can be seen, heard, and felt in classrooms. Teachers whose CMP has well-designed incentives can see students making choices to work toward accomplishing them. They can see students work together and hear students support each other in achieving goals. The classroom becomes a place where students feel more accountable and successful in meeting their learning goals and needs.

Instruction

The second component of the CMP is instruction. It has two parts: lessons and effective teaching practices. Classroom management and

Figure 2.2

Types of Incentives

Incentives can be defined as encouragers and reinforcers to accomplishing appropriate behaviors.

B. F. Skinner defines reinforcers as "reinforcing stimuli and . . . anything individuals experience or receive following a certain behavior that serves to strengthen that behavior" (quoted in Charles, 1999, p. 32). He divides reinforcers into the following four categories:

Social reinforcers: words, gestures, facial expressions, and behaviors that strengthen student behavior such as "Excellent," "Nice going," "I like that," or smiles, winks, or the "thumbs up" sign

Graphic reinforcers: check marks, stars, stickers

Activity reinforcers: activities students choose such as parties, games, free time, talk time, extra recess, free reading

Tangible reinforcers such as popcorn, candy, pencils, pens, decals, certificates, and happy grams instruction work together to enhance the teaching and learning processes. As it underlies the procedures; responsibilities; expectations; body language; cues; and instructional, preventive, supportive, and corrective strategies, the CMP supports teaching and learning and allows learning to happen.

Lessons

A CMP can help teachers plan and write lessons as it offers a kind of checklist to make sure they have included all the most important elements of effective instruction. These elements include clear objectives, an engaging presentation, active student involvement, good questioning and response techniques, varied activities addressing various learning styles, assessing student understanding, and individualized instructional strategies.

When teachers plan lessons, they determine the objectives of the lesson, decide how to introduce the topic, ascertain the most effective way to convey the information, and select activities that promote student understanding. The instructional strategies they choose capitalize on students' needs, interests, prior knowledge, and abilities.

The range of instructional and learning strategies teachers can use is broad and varied. Some instructional strategies include brainstorming, modeling and discussion, the use of graphic organizers, open-ended questions, and guided practice activities. Student learning strategies include individual, pair, and larger-group activities. These and other instructional and learning strategies for both individual students and the entire class are discussed in greater depth in Chapters 4 and 5.

In addition to strategies and techniques, teachers must have a way to assess the success of a lesson. Assessing refers to observing and collecting information about each student's understanding of the lesson. Students should also learn to assess their own learning. The teacher must give students the opportunity to evaluate themselves, and the CMP outlines the ideas and strategies that promote self-evaluation.

Success-building strategies increase students' participation and effort in learning and behaving more appropriately. These strategies range from giving thorough reviews before tests to using portfolios for assessment purposes. An understanding of Howard Gardner's (1993) multiple intelligences helps teachers develop success-building strategies for alternative-style learners. These and other strategies are discussed in Chapter 5.

Teachers must also have a plan for the use of classroom technology such as computers and video and audio equipment. Other resources available for classroom use include newspapers, transparencies, games, maps, globes, pictures, reference books, pamphlets, posters, manipulatives, and the human element—guest speakers. The process of creating the CMP requires teachers to think through ahead of time what resources are needed and available to teach the curriculum, and plan better use of these resources.

Effective teaching practices

Specific teacher behaviors and practices not only enhance instructional time and student learning, but they can also reduce discipline problems, decrease interruptions, and minimize student off-task behaviors. The effectiveness of classroom management becomes apparent when it creates the atmosphere needed for students to learn and for the class to work together. Simply put, learners need a positive classroom atmosphere and a teacher who offers positive reinforcement and support. Other effective teaching behaviors include having a positive attitude, building positive relationships among classmates, fostering student social skills, developing preventive and supportive discipline strategies, promoting problem-solving and decision-making skills, and encouraging student self-control.

Classroom management can have its greatest impact in the prevention of classroom discipline problems. Classroom management is found in the strategies teachers choose to prevent classroom or student situations or problems from occurring or escalating and the strategies they use to elicit support from the class and individual students in situations of frustration, confrontation, and intervention.

Both preventive and supportive discipline strategies begin with developing a sense of community in the classroom. Teachers must work to get students to like each other, work and learn together, and be accountable for how the class works. They must also work to get students to like them and to work for and learn from them. Establishing positive relationships and providing a student-centered, user-friendly, and risk-free environment becomes a teacher and a class responsibility. The CMP can structure the ideas, strategies, and procedures for how the class operates and how the class and individual students respond.

For example, a teacher can teach students a signal to use to express frustration so the teacher can go to the student immediately before the situation reaches a boiling point. The CMP can include procedures to reduce frustration such as allowing students to ask a buddy for help or allowing them a time-out so they can remove themselves from the situation for needed perspective. In times of confrontation, the class motto and policy can assist students in making good behavior choices and having a commitment to solving the problem. Because rules and consequences have been developed by the class, they are easier for students to follow and accept. Peer support, approval, and expectations help prevent and assist in solving many difficult and time-consuming classroom situations.

Students learn more and behave better in classrooms that meet their basic needs, and the need to belong is important to all members of the class. But often students' social skills are underdeveloped or they don't have a collective sense about working together for the common good. Strategies such as discussing and debating social issues, expressing personal opinions, reviewing current events, evaluating pros and cons of an issue, and employing conflict resolution methods can help students develop social skills and see the classroom as a community.

Conflict resolution methods are techniques the class develops for solving problems, preventing fighting, reducing tattling, and just getting along together. To solve problems, for example, teachers might give students procedures such as "Ask three before me," in which students ask three other students for their opinions and help to make a decision. A procedure to prevent fighting might include teaching students first, to back off; second, to leave the other student's space; and third, to count to 10. A procedure to prevent tattling might include listing this problem on the agenda for discussion at the next class meeting.

Regular class meetings give students an opportunity to take responsibility for the way the class works and the way each student works in the classroom. In class meetings, students make decisions, solve problems, and agree to make changes to improve classroom situations. Nelsen, Lott, and Glenn (2000) suggest training the class in the eight building blocks for effective classroom meetings: forming a circle, giving compliments, creating an agenda, developing communication skills, learning about realities, recognizing misbehaviors, practicing role-playing, and focusing on non-punitive solutions.

Linked with conflict resolution techniques are problem-solving and decision-making strategies and self-management behaviors that help students develop self-control. Any ideas, procedures, or tasks students can implement without teacher assistance give them a sense of independence, autonomy, and feelings of importance. Students need opportunities to learn how to behave in school, how to act in public and private situations, and how to be responsible people and citizens. A procedure such as the personal problem/solution plan (PPSP), which is a way to respond to confrontation with another person, teaches students self-control. The steps of the PPSP are first, to ignore the other person; second, to ask the person politely to stop; third, to ask the person to stop in a loud voice so others hear; and, finally, to ask a teacher or adult for help solving the problem (Bosch & Kersey, 2000, pp. 66–67). Such strategies provide both teachers and students with methods to resolve conflicts. Kohn (1996) suggests that teachers must work toward providing supportive environments in which students are included as collaborators in solving class problems.

Evaluation

While necessary, the third component of the CMP is one both students and teachers often find disagreeable. Evaluation conjures thoughts of subjectivity and unfairness. It is too often an active, threatening, and coercive component in classrooms. With the help of the CMP, and its clear outline of the grading scheme, students not only come to understand the grading process and procedures, they also feel they have some effect on their grades.

Professional Development

Professional development activities—the fourth component of the CMP—are planned opportunities to think about teaching in general, recall a specific lesson, or think about how to help an individual student. The importance of engaging in continuous reflective practice to advance or improve one's teaching effectiveness is recognized by many researchers (Ball, 2000; Cochran-Smith & Lytle, 1999; Loughran & Russell, 1997). One aspect of professional development is monitoring one's own teaching practices. Reflective practices may include journal writing, and planning quiet, focused thinking time. Teachers can periodically plan to videotape lessons and then review them alone, with a peer or mentor. Videotaping provides an opportunity to view one's teaching and identify areas needing improvement. Meeting with colleagues or a mentor, assigned or self-selected, can improve reflective practices. A mentoring relationship with an experienced teacher is seen as a way to reform teaching (Little, 1990). Participation in school inservice activities, taking college courses, and attending conferences provide other opportunities for professional development.

Teachers can monitor their teaching and classroom management to learn more about what they are really like as teachers; how they teach, manage, and interact with students; and how to achieve greater teacher effectiveness and learner success. Completing the self-evaluation activities in Chapter 3 and the observations in Chapter 4 will help teachers learn more about their teaching and how to manage classrooms that work.

3

Introspection: Getting in Touch With Your Teaching Self

Jennifer Hansen, the newest faculty member at Jacobs Middle School, entered the faculty lounge, placed the stack of papers she was carrying on the couch, and plopped down beside the pile. Kate Weber looked up from her writing when her young friend let out a huge sigh.

"Whew!" Jennifer exclaimed. "Thank heavens this day is over."

"Rough one?" Kate asked.

"That is an understatement. It seems everything went wrong today. I even had one student fall asleep during my lecture on the Constitution."

"We all have days like that. We just have to make sure they don't happen too often. That's why I have this," Kate said, and held up a spiral-bound notebook.

"What's that?" Jennifer asked, leaning forward to get a closer look.

"My teaching journal. I was just reflecting on a lesson I taught today that didn't go as well as I'd hoped."

"You're writing about it?" Jennifer asked, incredulously. "I don't want to think about this day ever again. In fact, I just want to forget it ever happened. It's done. It's over. That's that."

"Then how will you fix it?"

"Fix it?"

"Ever hear the saying, 'Those who cannot remember the past are condemned to repeat it'?"

"Sure. George Santayana. But tomorrow's another day. I'll start fresh then."

"So you know what went wrong?"

"Oh, sure," Jennifer grinned. "The weather is getting warmer. My students were thinking about baseball and in-line skating. They weren't interested in the Bill of Rights."

"Well, the weather's going to keep getting warmer. Of course, you could wait until fall to get their attention again . . . or you could think now about ways to get them interested in the Bill of Rights."

Suddenly Jennifer stopped smiling. "You're serious, aren't you? How often do you write in that journal?"

"Every day," replied Kate.

"But you've been teaching, what, eight years? Don't you have all your lessons planned out? Don't you teach the same lessons each year?"

"Well, yes, each year I cover American History from the Pilgrims landing at Plymouth Rock to the Gulf War, so the topics are the same, but the lessons themselves aren't. Each class is different, students change every year—how can my lessons stay the same?" Kate queried.

"Wow, I had no idea. Looks like I'm the one getting a valuable lesson today. So tell me about this reflecting idea. What exactly do you do?"

"Every day I make notes to myself on two things that worked that day and two things that didn't. I also jot down something new I learned, whether it was something a student taught me or something the students and I discovered together."

Jennifer lifted a finger to stop her friend, reached hurriedly for a pad of paper and a pen, then with pen poised to write, she nodded for Kate to continue.

"You can reflect on your teaching in whatever way is comfortable for you. Sometimes I make a Venn diagram at the end of a unit. I poll students about what they liked about the unit, then in one circle I list what they liked and in the other circle what I liked, and I see what matches. Sometimes instead of writing, I'll sit down with a colleague and we'll discuss our day, just like we're doing now. We can learn a lot from each other, you know."

"Do you mind if I tell you about my lesson today?" Jennifer asked. "Maybe you can give me some pointers."

ANALYZE YOUR TEACHING SELF

The classroom management process begins with introspection, which eventually leads to the sort of reflection Kate and Jennifer discuss in the scenario above. Jennifer has realized that she must take the time to reflect on the lesson that didn't go well, but to be a truly effective teacher, Jennifer also needs to reflect on her strengths as a person and convert these to professional strengths, using them to improve her classroom and help her students get more out of their lessons.

Teachers need to analyze their personal and teaching selves because they need to be mindful of who they are and can be in a classroom. By learning more about themselves, teachers can enhance both their teaching and their classroom management skills. In this chapter, teachers complete a questionnaire to begin the classroom management process. The introspective nature of the questions helps teachers identify their attitudes, beliefs, goals, strengths, and weaknesses so they can incorporate them into their classroom management plans. Once they recognize their personal strengths and weaknesses, they can use their strengths as assets to classroom management and recognize their weaknesses as areas needing support in their CMP. The Reflection Questionnaire gives teachers a starting point from which to develop their personal CMPs. Thus, they first observe within, then they move to the next step in the classroom management process and observe without, reflecting on their teaching selves in action as described in Chapter 4.

The purpose of this introspection is to ensure the CMP fits the teacher. The CMP can work only if the teacher feels comfortable with it. While one teacher's plan may share many components with the plan of a teacher down the hall or even all the other fourth-grade teachers, ultimately, the teacher must personalize the plan for it to be successful.

The questionnaire also helps bridge the gap between one's personal self and teaching self. Many teachers think it best to keep their personal and professional lives separate, but truly effective teachers find ways to incorporate their personal style and interests into their classroom, and their answers on the Reflection Questionnaire can help them do that. A teacher who enjoys art or music can incorporate these subjects into lessons, making them more interesting for the teacher and, as a result, for students. Using different approaches also provides the variety that appeals to alternate-style learners who may have trouble with the verbal/linguistic, mathematical/logical bent of traditional lessons. Auditory learners, for example, might respond particularly well to lessons that incorporate music. Teachers with a flair for the dramatic might let students perform skits or conduct interviews to demonstrate their understanding of a particular lesson. Identifying his or her particular skills and talents is a teacher's first step toward using them to good effect in the classroom.

REFLECTION QUESTIONNAIRE

The questions in the Reflection Questionnaire (see Figure 3.1) have no right or wrong answers. They are intended to get you thinking and promote further understanding of your teaching self—not just as you complete the questions but every day of your teaching life.

To stimulate your thinking about your own answers to these questions, read the discussion section that follows, which includes how other teachers have responded to the questions. Take the time to consider the discussion questions as well, to help you delve deeper into the question and your answers.

DISCUSSION OF THE REFLECTION QUESTIONNAIRE

1. What does the term classroom management *mean to you?*

Heide, a practicing fourth-grade teacher for 30 years, describes classroom management as "those skills needed by a teacher to establish and maintain a learning environment in which students are taught to be independent and accountable as they assume increasing responsibility for their own learning and conduct."

Shreve, a practicing teacher after one year of teaching, writes, "Classroom management isn't how quiet your room is or how frightened your students are into behaving, but rather how motivated and interdependent your students are in their work. Classroom management is teamwork."

Often, teachers define classroom management in terms of what they think others think it means. For example, if the principal stresses that classroom management simply means good discipline, the teacher must assume that definition to fulfill the principal's expectations and, of course, receive a good evaluation. However, that meaning may limit the school term's potential and, ultimately, a teacher's potential to be effective in a classroom.

To begin to understand the term classroom management, a teacher must separate the term from the literature and what others think it means, and find her or his own definition of this term. Ask yourself what this term means to you. To have classroom management operate in how you teach and in how your class works, the definition must be yours. Only then can you plan for classroom management, implement a CMP, and reflect on its improvement.

When you respond to question 1, record what classroom management means to you. Be careful not to let the literature or what others think cloud your true thoughts on what this term means to you. Also think about those classroom management skills Heide refers to that teachers need to create and maintain a learning environment. Which of these skills do you possess? Which skills do you wish to improve upon? Do you agree with Heide's definition?

Next, consider Shreve's description of classroom management. In what way is your response similar? In what way does your response differ? As an observer, what would you expect to see and hear in Shreve's classroom? How does your classroom compare with your image of Shreve's classroom? Do you wish any of these aspects were operating in your classroom? Why or why not? After envisioning Shreve's classroom, has your definition of classroom management changed at all?

2. Reflect on your philosophy of education. Write five "I believe" statements about teaching.

Jack, who has been teaching high school chemistry for five years, answered in the following way:

> *"1. I believe that as a teacher I should act as a coach, helping my students find the answers on their own, not feeding them the answers.*

Figure 3.1

Reflection Questionnaire

1. What does the term *classroom management* mean to you?

2. Reflect on your philosophy of education. Write five "I believe" statements about teaching.

3. List at least five of your strengths. Think about both personal strengths and talents. Circle those that particularly apply to classroom teaching.

4. Ask several family members and friends to tell you what they like best about you, and list their responses below. Note responses similar to yours.

5. List your weaknesses. Circle those the CMP may need to support and explain why.

6. List the most important qualities you wish to foster in your students.

7. How do you introduce yourself to the class? Write a short paragraph that you would use to introduce yourself to your class. Would you use "props," play music, or draw on the board?

8. Complete a concept map on "What Is Good Teaching?"

9. Write a brief paragraph on how you will make a difference in the lives of your students.

10. Find and copy a favorite quote, poem, or story that conveys an understanding of your teaching self. Explain why you chose it.

Source: Copyright © 2006 by Corwin Press. All rights reserved. Reprinted from *Planning Classroom Management*, 2nd edition, by Karen Bosch. Thousand Oaks, CA: Corwin Press, www.corwinpress.com. Reproduction authorized only for the local school site or nonprofit organization that has purchased this book.

Note: An electronic copy of this form may be found at corwinpress.com. Use the Product Search function to locate the *Planning Classroom Management* page. Then click on "Sample Chapters/Additional Materials" for a modifiable copy of the form.

2. *I believe teaching is the single most important profession, and I should strive daily to ensure my students know I feel this way so they respect the profession as well.*

3. *I believe students can instruct each other, sometimes better than I can instruct them, so group activities are valuable.*

4. *I believe that a student who feels respected, heard, and cared for will learn better and be better than a student who feels like a number in a grade book.*

5. *I believe that to teach people well, you must have an understanding of how people learn, so it is important to stay abreast of theories of cognition."*

The purpose of this activity is to remind you why you wanted to become a teacher and what you hoped to bring to the profession. Many people become teachers because of a teacher they once had. That teacher made a difference in their lives and the lives of other students. Perhaps this teacher made learning fun or was someone who showed students how much he or she cared about them. Teachers often begin their careers with a goal to be like their favorite teacher, with a strong commitment to the profession, and with a passion to make a unique difference. But amid all the classroom responsibilities and with the passage of time, these aspirations, along with remaining true to their teaching selves, get placed on the back burner and sometimes even forgotten.

Reflecting on teaching and writing the "I believe" statements put these goals back into focus and reaffirm priorities. These statements reflect who you are and who you can be as a teacher. They define your teaching self and can establish your role in planning and implementing classroom management when you incorporate your beliefs throughout the CMP in the ideas, strategies, and behaviors you choose. After writing the "I believe" statements, ask yourself how you can make sure they are working in your classroom. Find places in the CMP to address the "I believe" statements. They may appear in the class motto, the rules, procedures, and cues; your lesson plans; the instructional strategies and grading scheme you choose; or even in how you use reflection time.

Jack's statement, "I believe that a student who feels respected, heard, and cared for will learn better and be better than a student who feels like a number in a grade book," might be found in his CMP under a class rule such as "Respect must be earned and must be mutual." It might also appear under consequences, where he requires students to complete a behavior log when given a "time-out" consequence; under routines and procedures, where he has planned ways students can seek help by holding once-a-week help sessions, using a "buddy" system, holding class meetings, and assessing the class climate with a daily or weekly survey; under teaching practices, where he lets students use a "pass or play" option during question-and-answer sessions, where he outlines his responses for partially correct answers as well as incorrect ones, and where he plans student-success strategies; and under evaluation, where his grading plan encourages extra effort because he allows extra credit and rewrites and he averages grades on two or more assignments.

Assuring that your CMP mirrors your beliefs makes the plan easier to implement and makes its outcome more satisfying. The CMP helps you be who you are and who you want to be in the classroom.

As you read Jack's "I believe" statements, ask yourself what you would expect to see and hear in Jack's classroom. Do you agree with all Jack's "I believe" statements? Are any similar to what you have written? Identify the similarities.

3. List your strengths.

Include both personal strengths and talents. Circle those that apply to effective classroom teaching.

4. Interview family members.

Ask several family members and friends to tell you what they like best about you, and list their responses below. Circle those that apply to teaching, and note responses that are similar to yours.

5. List your weaknesses. Circle those the CMP may need to support.

Dawn has been teaching kindergarten for three years. Under strengths in question 3, she listed the following: assertive, tactful, caring, understanding, good listener, honest, open-minded, efficient, and nonjudgmental. In addition, she added that her love of music—singing and piano playing in particular—is also a strength. She circled all her answers, believing they all apply to teaching.

When Dawn asked her family to tell what they like best about her (question 4), their responses included the following: nice, delightful personality, happy, and a winning smile.

Under weaknesses in question 5, Dawn wrote that she gets discouraged too easily, she is sometimes too sensitive, she can't say no, she tends to run herself dry by giving too much, and she can be impatient.

In developing her CMP, Dawn can capitalize on these identified strengths and find ways to support the weaknesses. She can use the information from questions 3 and 4 in getting to know herself better and learning how others see her. Consider the case of a preservice teacher who in her education classes was a happy, positive, friendly person. This made it all the more surprising when her professor observed her in the classroom and found her to be a stern, very negative, and unapproachable teacher. The teacher was unaware of the personality switch. It takes a toll being someone and something you are not.

Dawn listed "assertive" as her first strength. She must now ask herself, "What do I mean by assertive? How do I apply this strength in my classroom?" When she views what her family likes best about her, Dawn will see that it is not her assertiveness they mention but that she is a nice, happy person with a winning smile and personality. Dawn may need to get in touch with who she is in a classroom.

Your strengths must carry over into the classroom and be felt by the students. Dawn's CMP can reflect her strengths of being happy and nice and having a winning smile: it might include "Greeting the students at the door each morning," which would be a great way for Dawn to offer the winning smile and transmit her happy attitude to students, parents, other teachers, and all school personnel. She can display her positive attitude in the room decor, the class motto, and her relationships with students and parents.

Dawn also says she gets discouraged quickly, is too sensitive, can't say no, gives too much, and at times is impatient. The CMP can support her perceived weaknesses. To prevent discouragement from setting in, Dawn needs to plan reflection time weekly and, possibly, daily. During reflection, Dawn can start with the positive events that happened, then isolate one or two areas to work on, devising some strategies to try. Reflection can keep Dawn from feeling discouraged and allow her to see the bright side of classroom teaching.

Dawn can plan "canned" responses to those who make demands on her time to prevent getting overly involved and committed. Giving too much is a problem for most teachers. So much needs to be done, but they can regulate the *timing* of getting it all done. For example, Dawn may find calling parents at the beginning of the year to be a time-consuming task, but she can plan in her CMP how to get the calling done. She might phone the parents of just five students each week for the first 5 weeks of class to introduce herself, instead of attempting to call all of them the first few days or the first week of school.

To support her feelings of impatience, Dawn could note when those feelings occur and write into her CMP a procedure that eliminates this situation from happening over and over again. For example, if not getting students' attention is a source of her impatience, Dawn could create a cue that gets their attention quickly without her saying a word. If she gets impatient because she has to give directions over and over, Dawn could set up a direction-giving procedure. Maybe she finds herself becoming impatient at the end of the day; she could plan a fun activity she enjoys or she could read to students at the end of the day.

6. List the most important qualities you wish to foster in your students.

Kimberly, a preservice teacher, explains, "When I started the courses in education, I was unsure of my choice. I did not like school when I was young. I do, however, remember one good thing about school. I had one teacher who made me want to learn. She was interesting, fun, understanding, and strict all at the same time. Everyone loved her. Maybe we all knew she had a genuine interest in all of us. I am no longer unsure of my career in teaching. I know I want to reach those children who hate school. I want to give them something good to remember. I want to teach to reach a child who is just like I was."

Whether your goal is general ("I want to foster in students a lifetime love of learning.") or specific ("I want students to see that physics is fascinating and fun!"), look for ways to build that goal into your CMP. Perhaps under Instruction, you will devise lesson plans that show students they already know more about physics than they realize (Did they know in-line skates work by means of friction and inertia?). Or by using the Internet to communicate with a classroom in Norway, your students will want to learn more about geography, languages, and the people and cultures of other lands throughout the world. If your goal is for students to be good citizens of the world, develop rules that teach them respect, honesty, and tolerance.

Identifying possible strengths and weaknesses in others sometimes helps one see inside oneself. Reflect on Kimberly's statement, and list some possible strengths and weaknesses of this teacher. Then evaluate your response to this question. Do you perceive strengths you can capitalize on or weaknesses requiring support?

7. How do you introduce yourself to the class?

Les, a practicing teacher, writes, "For 13 years, I labored away at an occupation I thoroughly detested. Unhappiness with work finally permeated every aspect of my life. Consequently, at 34 years of life, I made a commitment to find a career in which I could completely immerse myself, to enjoy and to love. Already possessing a master's degree, I returned to college at the undergraduate level to complete a teaching certificate. I had correctly sensed that there was no better profession for me than teaching.

Teaching has provided me the opportunity to share my love and appreciation for life with others. I am told that the energy I carry into the classroom reverberates off the walls and penetrates the hearts and minds of the students entrusted to me. Magically, they seem to become contagiously wrapped up in my enthusiasm and begin to believe that they can achieve their dreams."

First impressions are very important and no less so for teachers introducing themselves to their class for the first time. Les, the teacher who wrote the preceding statement, likely has a dynamic, exciting way to present his teaching self to his class. Remember that the introduction will be students' first and, likely, lasting impression. If one of your strengths is creativity, use this strength in your introduction. If you are an athlete or have a special interest or hobby, build that into the introduction. Use props or costumes. Dawn can plan an introduction around her love of singing and piano playing. Kim could share her personal experience of not liking school. The introduction is the icebreaker and the relationship builder.

If you are a preservice teacher, think about how you want your students to regard you in that first impression, then write in detail how you will introduce yourself to the class for the first time. If you are a practicing teacher, consider how you introduce yourself. Do you introduce yourself the same way every year? If yes, do you get the same response every year? Would you like to change students' response? What do you think students think of you? Is this the impression you want them to have? If not, what would you like them to think of you?

8. Complete a concept map on "What Is Good Teaching?"

Jennifer, the young teacher from the beginning of the chapter, had written a philosophy of education statement while still in college, in preparation for employment interviews, but the statement was merely full of theories of cognition and name dropping of key education theorists. She had not revised the statement since she'd actually begun teaching and had a class of her own. Jennifer was surprised to learn that Kate fills out the Reflection Questionnaire at least every two years. When Kate shared her most recent answers, Jennifer found herself nodding in agreement. "That's the way I feel, too, only I don't think I realized I felt that way until I heard you say it." That evening, Jennifer went home and completed the questionnaire. Her concept map looked like Figure 3.2.

Begin the concept map with a circle and put "Good Teaching" in the center as in the example shown. List ideas and strategies at the end of the spokes that radiate from this center circle. From these, think about how you might accomplish these ideas and concepts and the strategies you might use to do so.

This concept map is a quick way to think about what constitutes good teaching. Use the concept map when writing the CMP. Support the ideas, concepts, and strategies listed throughout the CMP in your choices of room arrangement, rules, procedures, cues, and so on.

9. Write a brief paragraph on how you will make a difference in the lives of your students.

The purpose of this exercise is to reaffirm your role in and your responsibility and commitment to teaching. Putting these thoughts in writing is somewhat like a contract. Consider incorporating these thoughts into your introduction to the class or into a class motto such as "Make a difference!" Completing this activity can shed some light on why teaching is important, and the CMP takes on more significance because it becomes the tool for making a difference.

10. Find and copy a favorite quote, poem, or story that conveys an understanding of your teaching self.

The purpose of this activity is to take something away from this exercise that serves as a tangible reminder to keep in touch with your teaching self. Many people have favorite quotes, stories, poems, sayings, songs, verses, and memories that provide inspiration, motivation, challenge, comfort, encouragement, and hope. People keep them on their desks or walls, in journals or on the pages of a lesson plan book, or folded and tucked in a special place—perhaps in a billfold, or a drawer. The purpose of finding the quote, story, poem, saying, or song is to inspire you to stay on the path and feel good about your teaching self and each teaching day.

For Further Introspection

From the point of view of an observer of your classroom, write the ideal observation. What would you like a "review" of your classroom to say? How close is your classroom to this ideal?

Take each aspect the review mentions. Place a star next to those statements you feel that you have achieved and that an observer visiting your

Figure 3.2

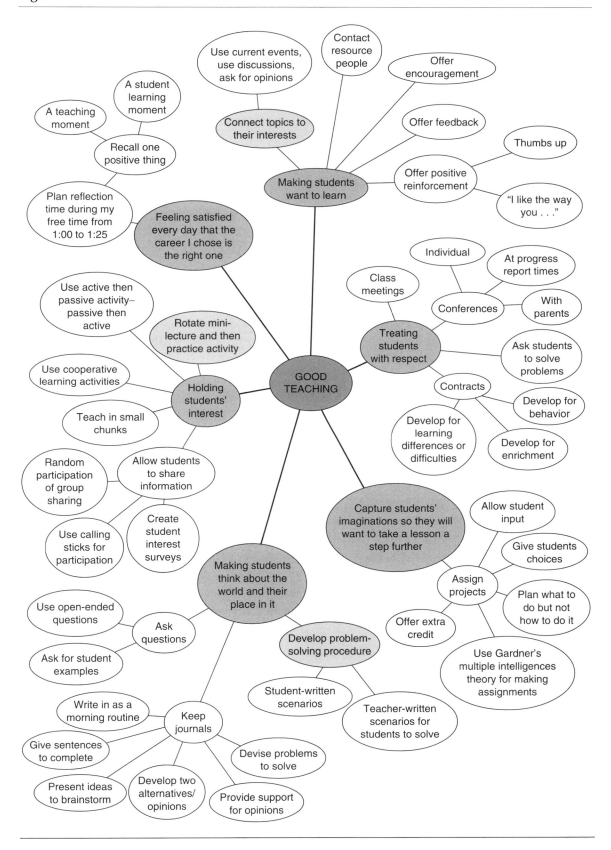

classroom tomorrow would note. Place an X next to those statements an observer might make on a good day or aspects you have experienced but not consistently. Place an O next to any observation an observer of your classroom is not likely to make. Why do you think this item does not exist in your classroom? What steps might you take to have this occur? Think about how you might construct your CMP to promote these events in your classroom.

INTROSPECTION AND REFLECTION AS AN ONGOING PROCESS

As Jennifer learned in the prologue to this chapter, being introspective and reflecting on past experience and present goals is important and necessary. Whether this reflection takes the form of solitary journal writing or conversations with colleagues, teachers should devote a portion of their day and their week to taking stock of the successes and failures in their classroom, both those of instruction and of management. Success breeds more success, and failures (problems) left unattended grow. Teachers need to celebrate effective teaching and learning successes to maintain job satisfaction, but a vital part of effective teaching is being a reflective teacher, a problem solver, an experimenter, and—always—a student of the art and science of teaching and learning.

Jennifer also learned that introspection is an ongoing process throughout one's career. Such reflection improves teacher effectiveness and learner success. Understanding and reflecting on your teaching self creates opportunities to stay mindful of who you are in a classroom and who you want to be in a classroom and why. Only then can the CMP become the window of possibilities and the conscience of effective teaching, and provide you with the impetus to change and the courage to keep trying.

Remember that you will change just as students change. Every year, complete the Reflection Questionnaire, answering each question again. You may be surprised at how your answers change. The exercise is a way for you to keep in touch with your teaching self and see how your views and values change and how these changes affect the classroom and the way you teach.

4

Classroom Observation

While his students work in their cooperative learning groups on their lab assignments, ninth-grade biology teacher Cliff Bosler takes a few minutes to take stock of the classroom. At one time, he kept a checklist in the back of his grade book of what to observe, but he has done this now so many times, he no longer needs the list.

He watches as students go from one lab activity to another and gauges the traffic pattern. He confirms that the quiet activities are grouped together in one area while the discussion groups meet in another part of the room near noisier activities. He looks to make sure students have enough room to conduct their experiments—room for all the equipment they need plus room for their notebooks. He checks to see that they have plenty of supplies to repeat experiments if necessary and that additional supplies are accessible to them.

As he moves among the students, he makes mental notes about the experiments that seem to hold their interest longest and most consistently. He listens carefully to their questions, assessing patterns. Is there one experiment with which all students seem to have difficulty? Is it a particularly complicated experiment, or are the instructions poorly written?

He watches the interaction among students in the groups in which he has placed them. He makes sure each group member participates in the activity, each performing his or her assigned role such as note-taker or timekeeper.

Cliff uses his time as seventh-period study hall monitor to jot down his observations for the day. Once a year, he supplements his observation with a videotape of the class. The tape allows him to review the class later in depth and with the luxury of distance and time. He keeps these tapes because they provide him with a visual history of how he and his classes change over the years, and he enjoys having a visual record of his students.

THE ROLE OF OBSERVATION IN THE CLASSROOM MANAGEMENT PROCESS

Observation is the second step of the classroom management process. The introspection required in Chapter 3 also prepares teachers to become more acute observers in classrooms, including their own. The purpose of this chapter is to help teachers identify specific practices, behaviors, and strategies at work in a colleague's classroom or their own.

In addition, this chapter offers an Observation Guide to help teachers see, hear, and feel what makes a classroom work, talk about why it works, and record how it works. Most observers discover that management can operate unobtrusively in classrooms. The classroom management Observation Guide provides a systematic and focused approach to observing classroom management in a classroom.

An Important Note About Observing a Classroom and Its Management

While a universally agreed-upon definition of classroom management does not exist among those associated with education, many teachers, parents, and administrators base their definition of classroom management on how students behave and judge a teacher's effectiveness based on this behavior. A quiet class with students in their seats doing their work suggests to them that a teacher is effective and worthy of a good evaluation. Evaluators are far less likely to expend the effort to judge a teacher's performance on a much more important basis—whether students are learning. For example, teachers seldom use cooperative learning activities if they know they will be observed by a principal. Classrooms may appear noisy and disorganized during cooperative learning activities, and old stereotypes of the ideal classroom are likely to prevail, to the detriment of the evaluation.

Observers must learn to evaluate teaching and learning, and the first step to a more meaningful evaluation is to consider "learning noise." All classrooms have learning noise. It is observed readily when students work in cooperative learning situations, read aloud, and help and teach others. Observing learning noise is a way to evaluate learning. Learning can be evaluated if a teacher or administrator looks for it, hears it, and feels student "getting it," but he or she can't do this unless students talk; move around; and think, share, work, and learn together. This chapter asks educators to shed long-held perceptions and move past the stereotype of the appearance of classroom management—desks in rows, students in their seats, no-talking classrooms—and learn to observe classroom management as a process that includes promoting and improving learning.

HOW TO CONDUCT OBSERVATIONS

Preservice teachers can begin to observe and document the classroom management process during teacher education courses and the early field experiences required in teacher preparation programs. Later they can observe their own classroom, as can practicing teachers. Practicing teachers can also look to their colleagues. By observing their own and others' classrooms and using the classroom management Observation Guide to help them focus on the specifics that make up classroom management, teachers can understand that a good classroom doesn't just happen: a plan must be developed that ensures it. Observing practicing teachers who have a classroom management plan provides valuable training for both preservice and practicing teachers, allowing them the opportunity to witness and understand the value of classroom management and obtain ideas to take back to their own classrooms.

Observations can provide many opportunities for professional growth and development. In addition to the Observation Guide, videos and journals can aid the observation process. Often, it takes all these documentation tools to understand fully how the teacher and the class work and how they work together and support each other. While teachers performing a self-observation can complete much of the Observation Guide after they have taught a class, to respond fully and honestly to each of the sections, they may want to have the class videotaped. In addition to allowing teachers to observe their classroom more fully and with the luxury of some distance, the videotaping process helps them become accustomed to observers in their room, whether they are colleagues, administrators, or parents.

An additional note on videotaping: Some schools do not allow videotaping of classrooms. Others may allow it if teachers have permission slips signed by parents stating the purpose and use of the tape.

Be Prepared

To prepare to observe a colleague's classroom, follow these guidelines:

- Make several copies of the Observation Guide. Place guides, extra paper, and pencils in a folder or notebook. Read over the guide before the observation takes place so the areas you are to complete are fresh in your mind.
- You will complete the Observation Guide through a combination of observation and interview, so schedule time with the teacher outside of the classroom to clarify certain items and complete those items not observable in their classroom such as the teacher's reflection practices.
- Make plans with the teacher to conduct the observation, and schedule the day and time for the observation. Give the teacher a copy of the Observation Guide and explain that you will complete the guide during your visit. Many teachers may be concerned about the writing taking place while they are teaching, so assure them that you will be as unobtrusive as possible. Plan to take notes or bullet ideas during the observation and expand on them after the visit.
- Ask the teacher for a copy of the seating chart and the lesson plan for the day you will visit.

- Ask for a place in the room to conduct the observation that would be least obtrusive and distracting to students.
- During the observation, record information for each component of the Observation Guide. Write in lists and short phrases or sentences.
- Take time to see, hear, and feel the management operating in the classroom.
- If you are unable to observe some items, leave them blank. After the observation, discuss the missing items with the teacher.

Do not limit your observation to teachers who teach the same grade or subject you do. Collect data from teachers of different subjects and in different settings such as primary, intermediate, middle, or secondary grades.

Remember that through observations, teachers can learn both what works and what doesn't. Equipped with the expertise gained from having seen the modeling of both effective and ineffective teaching, teachers can begin to reach their potential and learn to be effective in any situation, applying whatever a particular classroom requires.

THE OBSERVATION GUIDE

This section accompanies the Observation Guide and is designed to help teachers understand what to look for (observe). The information applies to observation of both a colleague's and a teacher's own classroom. The Observation Guide comprises four parts: Observing Classroom Organization (Figure 4.1), Observing Instruction (Figures 4.2 and 4.3), Observing Evaluation (Figure 4.4), and Observing Reflective Teaching Practices (Figure 4.5).

Overview: The Initial Impression

In *Beyond Discipline: From Compliance to Community*, Kohn (1996) suggests that teachers take time in a faculty meeting to define the word *community* in a school context. He suggests that they identify what an observer would see, hear, and feel in a place that is described as a community. The See, Hear, Feel method of observation is essentially one's first impression of how a classroom works. Classroom management is seen in the room arrangement, bulletin boards, and procedures. It is heard in the conversations between teacher and student and among classmates and in the working/learning noise level in the room. It is felt in the tone of the classroom—the sense of willingness, positiveness, and encouragement observed, or simply the feeling an observer gets being in the classroom (see also Figure 4.6). In your first moments in the classroom, use the See, Hear, Feel method of observation, and write what you see, hear, and feel in the classroom.

Part I: Observing Classroom Organization

1, 2, 3. The first sign of classroom management is in the classroom environment. Much in the physical arrangement either supports classroom

(Text continued on page 36)

Figure 4.1

Observation Guide

PART I: OBSERVING CLASSROOM ORGANIZATION

1. Describe what you see and hear in the classroom and how you feel about what is taking place.

2. Draw or describe the room arrangement and an interesting bulletin board idea.

3. Write the class motto.

4. List the classroom rules as well as rights, expectations, and responsibilities.

5. Describe a few classroom routines and procedures.

6. List the classroom consequences, and describe any consequences you observe.

7. Describe a few individual or group incentives the teacher uses.

8. Describe ways students can change the structure of the classroom.

9. What verbal and nonverbal cues does the teacher use, and how do students respond to them?

Source: Copyright © 2006 by Corwin Press. All rights reserved. Reprinted from *Planning Classroom Management*, 2nd edition, by Karen Bosch. Thousand Oaks, CA: Corwin Press, www.corwinpress.com. Reproduction authorized only for the local school site or nonprofit organization that has purchased this book.

Note: An electronic copy of this form may be found at corwinpress.com. Use the Product Search function to locate the *Planning Classroom Management* page. Then click on "Sample Chapters/Additional Materials" for a modifiable copy of the form.

Figure 4.2

Observation Guide

PART II: OBSERVING INSTRUCTION: LESSONS

10. What "hook" did the teacher use to begin the lesson and capture students' interest? Was the hook effective?

11. Explain how the teacher makes lesson objectives clear to students.

12. Describe instructional strategies the teacher uses that you found effective.

13. Do all students participate in the lesson? On the seating chart, place an X on students called on to answer questions during the lesson.

14. Record a few questions the teacher asks students during the observed lesson, and provide examples of how the teacher responds to student answers.

15. Record how much response time the teacher gives students to answer a question: approximately _____ seconds.

16. Explain how the teacher gives directions to the class.

17. How does the teacher assess student learning during a lesson?

18. What success-building strategies does the teacher use?

19. On the chart showing room arrangement, sketch the teacher's movement during the lesson.

20. How does the teacher close a lesson?

21. Describe the teacher's use of resources.

Source: Copyright © 2006 by Corwin Press. All rights reserved. Reprinted from *Planning Classroom Management,* 2nd edition, by Karen Bosch. Thousand Oaks, CA: Corwin Press, www.corwinpress.com. Reproduction authorized only for the local school site or nonprofit organization that has purchased this book.

Figure 4.3

Observation Guide

PART II: OBSERVING INSTRUCTION: EFFECTIVE TEACHING PRACTICES

22. Give examples of how the teacher praises and encourages students.

23. Observe and record some examples of how the teacher talks to the students and how the students talk to the teacher and to each other.

24. Give examples of feedback the teacher gives students.

25. How does the teacher respond to disruptive behavior?

26. How does the teacher demonstrate high expectations for student learning?

27. Identify the strategies the teacher uses to develop and promote positive relationships with students, among classmates, and with parents.

28. What strategies does the teacher use to develop students' social skills?

29. Describe any problem-solving or decision-making skills students display.

30. Does the teacher regularly hold a class meeting? When and how is it conducted?

Source: Copyright © 2006 by Corwin Press. All rights reserved. Reprinted from *Planning Classroom Management*, 2nd edition, by Karen Bosch. Thousand Oaks, CA: Corwin Press, www.corwinpress.com. Reproduction authorized only for the local school site or nonprofit organization that has purchased this book.

Figure 4.4

Observation Guide

PART III: OBSERVING EVALUATION

31. Describe the teacher's grading scheme.

32. Does the teacher issue progress reports?

33. Do students have opportunities to impact their grades?

34. Does the teacher use the computer to record grades?

Source: Copyright © 2006 by Corwin Press. All rights reserved. Reprinted from *Planning Classroom Management*, 2nd edition, by Karen Bosch. Thousand Oaks, CA: Corwin Press, www.corwinpress.com. Reproduction authorized only for the local school site or nonprofit organization that has purchased this book.

Figure 4.5

Observation Guide

PART IV: OBSERVING REFLECTIVE TEACHING PRACTICES

35. Does the teacher schedule reflection time?

36. How does the teacher reflect on classroom and student problems, situations, and experiences?

37. Does the teacher keep a journal?

38. Does the teacher videotape the class for self-evaluation?

39. Does the teacher have a mentor?

40. Does the teacher participate in school inservice activities, take college courses, or attend conferences?

Source: Copyright © 2006 by Corwin Press. All rights reserved. Reprinted from *Planning Classroom Management*, 2nd edition, by Karen Bosch. Thousand Oaks, CA: Corwin Press, www.corwinpress.com. Reproduction authorized only for the local school site or nonprofit organization that has purchased this book.

Figure 4.6

First Impressions Count
What first impression would an observer to your classroom have? Reflect on the following statements:
What would an observer see in your classroom?
What would an observer hear?
How would an observer feel about what goes on in your classroom?

management or undermines it. Sketch what you see, such as the arrangement of furniture or an interesting bulletin board. If the class has a motto, write it down.

4, 5, 6. Classroom organization is seen next in the formulated policies, rules, routines and procedures, incentives, consequences, and cues. Look for a list of rules, rights, expectations, or responsibilities and copy them. If students have classroom jobs, provide some examples. Does a poster or sign identify these students and their responsibilities? In what ways are students recognized in the classroom—for example, student of the week, group of the day, birthday poster. All of this is physical evidence of how the teacher works, how the teacher and students work together, and how the classroom is expected to work.

Identify and describe a few observed classroom routines and procedures. Note particularly the routines established when students enter the classroom in the morning or for each bell or period, and the routines for ending the day or each bell or period. What procedure, for example, do students follow when they finish their work?

Classroom consequences usually appear on a poster or bulletin board; list them. If you observe consequences, note the amount of time and attention the teacher gives to disciplining a few students in the classroom while the majority of students are waiting to learn.

7. Describe a few individual and group incentives the teacher uses, such as no homework if students do well on in-class assignments or free reading time if everyone contributes to a class discussion. A marble jar may be used to support the "good" behavior of the class. This is a container that the teacher drops marbles into when she catches the class doing something good. The noise of dropping one or more marbles in the container provides positive reinforcement for all students. The class decides on what reward will be given when the container is full, so they work together to reach this goal. A reminder—no marbles are to be taken out of the container if a student or the class misbehaves. They have been earned by the class.

8. Look and listen for democratic ways students can change the structure of the classroom, such as through a suggestion board or box, dialogue journals, or scheduled class meetings.

9. Describe the teacher's use of cues to get students' attention, to get them into groups, or to signify the beginning of a lesson.

See Figure 4.1 for Part I of the Observation Guide.

Part II: Observing Instruction: Lessons

10, 11. Follow the teacher's lesson plan as he or she teaches. Pay particular attention to the manner in which the teacher teaches and students learn. Observe how the teacher captures students' interest—what "hook" does the teacher use to begin the lesson? Observe how the teacher engages students in the lesson and how he informs students of the lesson objectives. Observe how attentive students are during the lesson and how actively involved and engaged they are in learning the lesson.

12. Describe instructional strategies the teacher uses; for example, does the teacher use graphic organizers, guided practice activities, think-pair-share or cooperative learning activities (see also Figure 4.7)? If the teacher uses such strategies, provide details. If the teacher uses cooperative learning activities, how are the pairs or groups selected? Guided practice is any non-graded assignment in which students summarize what they know, write an example, or complete an exercise to practice what they have learned.

13. How does the teacher ensure that all students participate in the lesson? On the seating chart, place an X on students who are called on to answer questions during the lesson. Note students who are called on the most and which students are not called on at all. Write your conclusions. If student response is unequal, reflect on why this might be the case. What could a teacher do to ensure that all students participate and are called on?

14, 15. Observing how teachers question students and how students respond provides clues to how well students understand the topic or lesson. Record a few questions the teacher asks students during the observed lesson, and provide examples of how the teacher responds to a student in the following situations: when a student gives a correct answer to a question, when a student gives a partially correct answer, when a student gives an incorrect answer. Record how much time the teacher gives students to answer a question (see Figure 4.8).

16. In explaining how the teacher gives directions to the class, try to identify a consistent direction-giving procedure or pattern the teacher uses. Provide examples of any verbal advanced organizers (use of such terms as first, next, then, finally) the teacher uses when giving directions.

17. What techniques does the teacher use to assess student learning during a lesson? For example, does she stop periodically to question students about what she's taught? Does she scan the room for body language signals from students? Does she walk around while students are working to see if they understand the assignment? Consider also any opportunities the teacher provides for differentiated instruction, individualized instruction, or enrichment to meet the needs of all learners in the classroom. Describe specific techniques the teacher uses to meet the needs of diverse student populations.

Figure 4.7

Cooperative Learning

Cooperative learning is an instructional strategy that uses student groups to achieve learning goals. The idea is that as a group, students can learn more than they could alone—"Two heads are better than one!" In addition, the act of teaching each other results in increased understanding and retention. The strategy creates a more cooperative classroom because students must work together to achieve a desired outcome. As a result, they also acquire responsibility; self-esteem; and higher-level thinking, problem-solving, and social skills.

Many different types of instructional strategies fall under the general heading of cooperative learning. The idea underlying all cooperative learning activities is that group members work through an assignment until all group members understand and complete it successfully. All group members gain from the other members' efforts, and the group's success depends on every member's performance. Group members learn to depend on each other, and each rises to the occasion, recognizing that they can achieve their objectives only if each member of the group achieves his or her goal.

One popular cooperative learning technique is the think-pair-share strategy. It consists of three steps. In the first, students think about a question the teacher proposes; second, they discuss their thoughts with partners; and third, the pair shares their combined thoughts with the class.

Another effective cooperative strategy is called the Jigsaw I and II model, in which each group of four must complete an assignment together and that assignment has four parts (the number of members equals the number of parts). In Jigsaw II, each group member is assigned one of the four parts, and then the students are regrouped by parts (from a group to a subgroup and return to the original group). The Jigsaw II is sometimes referred to as the "experts group," as they provide important specific information to the basic group. For example, each group meets together to collect information from the social studies textbook (the teacher has prepared a graphic organizer for the group—Jigsaw I—to complete) that highlights the nation of China. The four parts of China that are to be explored are the demographics, economy and trade, culture, and politics. Each group member is then given a number from 1 to 4 that correspond to one of the areas. After a certain amount of time, the teacher asks that all ones (demographics), twos (economy and trade), etc., from all of the groups meet together as a subgroup to further discuss and complete a form pertaining to the specific area. After a certain amount of time, the teacher directs the subgroup members to return to their original groups and share the additional information learned. The original group must then incorporate that information into their graphic organizer. The teacher collects the group work and can grade the collective work—graphic organizer—by giving the members all the same grade, and can further provide individual assessment by collecting and giving individual grades for the form required for the members of the subgroups.

Cooperative learning teams are usually mixed by ability, motivation, and even gender and race. Cooperative learning necessitates rules and expectations for working and learning together; procedures for selection of group members and roles for members within the group; a direction-giving procedure for clarity of purpose and quality of work; time limits for efficiency; and evaluation for accountability and productivity. Teachers can add incentives to cooperative activities by giving group points for achievement and improvement on individual evaluations.

---

18. What are some success-building strategies the teacher uses? For example, does the teacher hold review sessions before tests? Describe opportunities the teacher provides for students to evaluate their own work, note progress, and plan for improvement. Does the teacher have

Figure 4.8

> **Patience Is More Than a Virtue**
>
> Response time, or wait time, is the time teachers allow for students to answer a question. Each learner is entitled to time to think before responding to a question. Research indicates that, on average, teachers wait only one second for a student to respond to a question before the teacher answers the question or calls on someone else (Rowe, 1974). Tobin (1987) reports that when teachers' wait time was greater than three seconds, students reached higher cognitive levels of learning. Jones and Jones (2004) suggest that a teacher wait at least five seconds. They cite Rowe who reports that when teachers increase their wait time, such advantages can occur: length and variety of students' responses increase, failure to obtain a response decreases, students' confidence increases, teacher-centered teaching decreases, and lower-achieving students contribute more (Jones & Jones, 2004). An easy way to ensure adequate response time is for the teacher to make eye contact and count slowly and silently, "one-one thousand, two-two thousand, three-three thousand," and so on.

---

students maintain a portfolio? Does the teacher or student select examples of the student's work to place in the portfolio?

19. On the seating chart the teacher has supplied, use arrows to sketch the teacher's movement during a lesson. Place a square around the spot the teacher occupies most often or returns to as he moves around the room. Are there some areas in the classroom that remain untouched by the teacher's travels? Does the teacher favor one area of the room? Determine if there is a pattern to the teacher's movement.

20. Closure to a lesson has a purpose just as the opening does. The teacher should ask students to summarize what they have learned. Closure must come from the students, not the teacher. How does the teacher encourage students to provide closure?

21. List the media, visual aids, and resources the teacher uses in the lesson. If the teacher uses the computer in the lesson, describe how. If the school has a computer lab, how does the teacher use the lab? How does the teacher use media, visual aids, and resources in the teaching of lessons?

See Figure 4.2 for Part II of the Observation Guide.

Part II: Observing Instruction: Effective Teaching Practices

22. Provide some examples of praise the teacher offers. Praise is positive reinforcement. If the teacher uses the positive ripple effect, provide an example. The positive ripple effect described by Kounin (1977) is heard in teacher responses such as, "I like the way the class, such as classmates Kathy, Jimmy, and John to name a few, has notebooks on the desk and all are ready to begin." Students hear that and quickly open notebooks and look ready to begin. How does the teacher offer encouragement to students? Encouragement differs from praise in that it can be offered to a student in the beginning, in the middle, and at the end of lessons and assignments.

Figure 4.9

> **Preventive Discipline Strategies**
>
> The use of eye contact and proximity are preventive discipline strategies—techniques teachers use to keep situations or problems from starting, continuing, or escalating. Kounin discusses "withitness" and "overlapping" as two important traits of teachers good in classroom discipline (cited in Charles, 1999). Withitness is anticipating what will happen before it happens; it is noticing, being aware and perceptive, having intuition—in essence, picking up on situations early. Teachers can demonstrate their awareness of classroom situations, their withitness, first with eye contact. The degree of eye contact can range from scanning the room to a prolonged stare while they continue teaching to stopping, staring, and waiting. Next, teachers can use proximity: they close the space between themselves and the problem or situation, moving into the student's space.
>
> Withitness is also collecting information to use later. For example, a teacher displaying withitness might say, "Johnny, that is the second time this week you have not completed your homework." Students recognize that the teacher knows and remembers. Jotting notes and keeping lists help teachers be more "with it."
>
> "Overlapping" refers to the ability to do more than one task at a time and be in two places at the same time. An example of this skill is monitoring four groups at a time or assisting one group while answering an individual's question. To enhance overlappingness, teachers should position themselves where they can keep the majority of students in view, scan the room frequently, move around the room, plan assistance procedures for projects and assignments, and teach students problem-solving strategies.

23. When observing and recording examples of how the teacher talks with the students and the students talk with the teacher and with other classmates, note the presence of positiveness or negativity, politeness or rudeness, and kindness or sarcasm.

24. Describe the oral and written feedback the teacher gives to help students improve the quality of their work or effort.

25. If the teacher uses eye contact and proximity to stop inappropriate behavior, describe the teacher's actions (see Figure 4.9). If the teacher ignores some behavior, describe a situation. How does the teacher foster student self-discipline and self-control?

26. How does the teacher demonstrate high expectations for student learning? For example, high expectations are seen in the teacher's body language (nodding of head with a wink) and nonverbal signals such as cues (thumbs up); they are heard in how the teacher asks questions and responds to answers—are the questions stated positively? Listen for statements like "I know you can do the job!"

27. How does the teacher promote positive relationships between herself and students, among classmates, and with parents? Ask the teacher if she uses activities such as get-acquainted games or interest surveys, and if he or she conducts student conferences. Try to determine how the teacher shows she cares about the students and how the students know the teacher cares.

Note when observing the classroom whether students get along and work together well. Some classrooms are filled with tattling, name-calling, negative remarks, and competition. In an effective classroom, an observer sees less competition, more cooperation, student smiles, and supportive remarks. Camaraderie, (group) cohesiveness, cooperative spirit, and a sense of community are the four Cs to positive relationships among classmates, and relationship building is the fourth R in classrooms.

Ask the teacher how she feels about working with parents. What strategies has the teacher found that have worked in reaching parents and gaining their support?

28. How does the teacher develop students' social skills? Many teachers teach lessons on social skills. They may lead discussions, make assignments, and have guest speakers talk to the class about skills needed to be successful, or they may read books to the class to stimulate discussions on areas of classroom relationships that need development.

29. Do students display any problem-solving or decision-making skills? Do they seem to follow a procedure to solve their problems or make more informed decisions?

30. Does the teacher regularly hold a class meeting? When and how is it conducted? Ask to observe such a meeting, or discuss with the teacher what takes place at the meeting.

See Figure 4.3 for the second half of Part II of the Observation Guide.

Part III: Observing Evaluation

31. Describe the teacher's grading scheme. For example, does he use a numeric grading scale? What weight does the teacher assign to certain activities? Do students have input in the grading plan? Does student effort affect the grading scheme? (When grading is responsive to students and their effort, students demonstrate more effort and thus, learn more.) Ask the teacher if you can see the grade book. A teacher might indicate grades in one color, quizzes in another.

Currently, many teachers maintain grades with the use of the computer and this seems to limit the students' immediate access to viewing grades. If a teacher provides opportunities for students to impact their recorded grades through rewrites and extra credit, the recording of this must be clear and orderly in the grade book or readily accessible and easily understood in a computer printout. Look for the homework policy, which may be posted, or discuss the policy with the teacher. What is the policy? Do students receive points for homework or outside tasks that can affect a grade? How much does homework count in the final grade? When and how is it collected? When is it considered late? If students have done it but forgotten it, when is the latest time they can turn it in to the teacher and still receive credit? Can students make up homework, tests, or quizzes if they are absent, and how long does a student have to make up the assignments?

32. Does the teacher issue progress reports? Explain the procedure, and ascertain the role of progress reports in the classroom. Does the progress report provide feedback to a student, or is it just a school requirement? Does the teacher use the progress report as an opportunity to discuss the progress with the student and share ideas that may help a student change the situation? Do students receive an update of grades intermittently for self-evaluation and self-monitoring? For example, are students able to view all their grades in the grade book or computer print-out, check to see if any assignments are missing, and make sure the teacher recorded the grades for each assignment correctly? Students can then see where the grades went up or down, see how the teacher arrived at the progress report grade, and do the math themselves to calculate and check their progress report grade.

33. Do students have opportunities to impact their grades by doing extra credit, rewriting papers, dropping a grade, completing special assignments, or by other means? Do students receive points for cooperative learning activities or projects that the teacher factors into the final grade?

34. Does the teacher use a computer software program to record student grades? Note the timeliness of entering the grades and the student accessibility to viewing their grades.

See Figure 4.4 for Part III of the Observation Guide.

Part IV: Observing Reflective Teaching Practices

35. Does the teacher schedule time during the school day or week to reflect on the day, lessons, and classroom management? Is time set aside to think about what went well and what areas need to be improved?

36, 37. How does the teacher reflect on classroom and student problems, situations, and experiences? Does the teacher plan time to meet with other teachers who teach at the same grade level or the same subject? If so, how often do they meet? For how long? What sort of topics do they discuss? Does the teacher observe other colleagues' classrooms? Does the teacher keep a journal? If so, how often does the teacher make an entry?

38. Does the teacher videotape his or her lessons periodically for self-evaluation or gain feedback from a peer review process? How does the teacher feel about videotaping? peer review?

39. Does the teacher have a mentor at the school? Do they meet at a regularly scheduled time?

40. Does the teacher participate in school inservice activities, take college courses, or attend conferences to learn new teaching skills?

See Figure 4.5 for Part IV of the Observation Guide.

Developing a Personal Classroom Management Plan

Kneeling between the rows of newly planted seeds and starts, Mary Williams inserted the last tomato plant in the hole she had dug, sat back on her heels, and looked over her garden. All she had to do was water the soil and let Mother Nature work her magic. But working in the garden had given Mary lots of time to think, and what she had thought about was her first year of teaching, which had ended a few weeks before. It had been an exciting year, a challenging year. She had loved her third-grade class at Wright Elementary, and except for a few minor incidents, she had thoroughly enjoyed her first year. Wright's principal, Bill Phillips, had visited her class several times, and in their meetings that followed his observations, he had both compliments and suggestions for improving her class. In their last meeting, Bill told her he was confident that many of the minor problems he saw would improve as she gained experience. Her style was engaging, he said, her lessons held students' interest, but her group work was weak, and she seemed undecided about the best way to handle disruptive behavior, perhaps, he said, because it was so infrequent.

But he was right. She was still not comfortable with cooperative learning activities, and she was not good at handling behavior problems. They threw her, and she felt herself losing confidence when such problems occurred. What's more, the students seemed to sense her uncertainty. Taking off her gardening gloves, Mary went into the house and pulled out a manila folder from a drawer in her desk. The folder contained information on creating a classroom management plan. "When school starts in the fall," Mary thought, "I will be ready." And she sat down with pen in hand and began to write her personal classroom management plan.

THE PERSONAL CMP

Evertson, Emmer, Clements, et al. (1989) remind teachers, "Good classroom management doesn't just happen. Smoothly running classrooms where students are highly involved in learning activities and that are free from disruption and chronic misbehavior do not happen accidentally" (p. xi). Indeed, such classrooms exist because teachers have a plan to make them happen and are prepared to carry out the plan and meet that goal.

When teachers develop a CMP, they integrate classroom management theory and practice into how they teach, how their students learn, and how their classrooms work. The CMP places this theory and practice into a structure that teachers can implement in a classroom, emphasizing teachers' strengths and supporting their weaknesses. The plan structures their teaching and student learning yet supports teacher and student autonomy and promotes a sense of community. The CMP maximizes instructional and learning time and minimizes interruptions, distractions, and disruptions. Classroom management, instruction, and teacher behavior interact to create a productive and positive learning environment (Brigham, Renfro, & Brigham, 1994).

The CMP reflects teachers' personality, experience, and skills and includes their own ideas, ideas and practices they have observed in effective classrooms, ideas they have read about in textbooks and professional journals, ideas from education courses, and ideas colleagues have shared. Teachers can learn from others, but they can't adopt someone else's teaching or managing style; teachers must write their own script. Educator Les Fortune says, "Ultimately, a teacher's classroom management style must become an extension of that educator's personality and philosophies combined with the chemistry of the students in the classroom. What works for one may not work for another." Merging the information from the introspection component in Chapter 3 and the observed information from the Observation Guide in Chapter 4, the teacher can begin to develop a personal classroom management plan (Figure 5.1). The CMP can now be personal, realistic, and filled with meaningful content and insights. Teachers can maintain their plan easily throughout the year because it supports who they are and what they want to be in a classroom.

COMPOSING A PERSONAL CMP

Getting Started

Collect the information recorded in Chapter 3 as well as the information collected from the Observation Guide completed in Chapter 4. Check or highlight all the items you want to include in the CMP. Look for ideas and strategies that complement your strengths and support your areas of weakness. For example, if discipline is not your strength, stress incentives in your plan. Choose only the consequences you believe you can implement consistently. If you are the type of person who gives second chances, choose a more liberal grading scheme. If you do not want to take time away from lessons to take roll or lunch count, plan the student jobs so students complete these tasks. If you thrive on organization, set up many routines, procedures, and policies for a scheduled, predictable day.

If you are a practicing teacher, your completed CMP may partially reflect what already goes on in your classroom. In other words, if you feel your classroom incentives work well, simply fill in the CMP with incentives you use currently. If you are a preservice teacher, fill in the CMP as if you are describing your classroom, even if it's only as it exists in your mind, using present tense. The following guidelines and questions will help you respond to each component of the CMP and understand how and why a component works. Note that the guidelines and questions are in present tense. For all teachers, describing your classroom in present tense helps you internalize your goals and see them as taking place today rather than in some uncertain future time.

Teaching Goal

The plan begins with a teaching goal. Look over the information recorded in Chapter 3 for help in writing this goal. Your teaching strengths; how others see you; your "I believe" statements; qualities you want to foster in your students; how you plan to make a difference in the lives of students you teach; and the quote, poem, or story you chose to reflect your teaching self all factor into this goal. Write the goal as one you want for yourself or for your students. This teaching goal sets the stage for developing other ideas in the CMP. For the time being, keep it a short-term goal—what you hope to accomplish this year, for example. Your goal may be specific—perhaps to focus on instructional strategies that appeal to alternate-style learners or to improve your relationship with parents. Or your goal may be more general—for example, to let your students know how important they and their education are.

CLASSROOM ORGANIZATION

Classroom Environment

Part of classroom environment involves not only making students feel comfortable and safe physically, it also includes creating an atmosphere that makes them feel emotionally secure and valued as persons. Students need to feel accepted and encouraged. They need to feel it's okay for them to take risks. They also need to feel respected and that their opinions and ideas are worthwhile.

(Text continued on page 52)

Figure 5.1

My Personal Classroom Management Plan

Teaching Goal(s) or Objective(s):

CLASSROOM ORGANIZATION

Classroom Environment

Draw or describe your room arrangement.

Sketch bulletin board ideas that you have seen or develop one bulletin board for your classroom.

Record class motto you are planning to use

Classroom Operation

Class Rules

1.

2.

3.

4.

5.

Source: Copyright © 2006 by Corwin Press. All rights reserved. Reprinted from *Planning Classroom Management*, 2nd edition, by Karen Bosch. Thousand Oaks, CA: Corwin Press, www.corwinpress.com. Reproduction authorized only for the local school site or nonprofit organization that has purchased this book.

Note: An electronic copy of this form may be found at corwinpress.com. Use the Product Search function to locate the *Planning Classroom Management* page. Then click on "Sample Chapters/Additional Materials" for a modifiable copy of the form.

Figure 5.1 (Continued)

My Personal Classroom Management Plan

Class routines and procedures

Class consequences

1.

2.

3.

4.

5.

Class incentives

Class cues

Source: Copyright © 2006 by Corwin Press. All rights reserved. Reprinted from *Planning Classroom Management*, 2nd edition, by Karen Bosch. Thousand Oaks, CA: Corwin Press, www.corwinpress.com. Reproduction authorized only for the local school site or nonprofit organization that has purchased this book.

Figure 5.1 (Continued)

My Personal Classroom Management Plan

INSTRUCTION

Lessons

Instructional strategies

Individualized instructional strategies

Assessment strategies

Questioning strategies

Examples of questions

Responses to students:

When a student gives a correct answer

When a student gives a partially correct answer

When a student gives an incorrect answer

Student self-evaluation opportunities

Source: Copyright © 2006 by Corwin Press. All rights reserved. Reprinted from *Planning Classroom Management*, 2nd edition, by Karen Bosch. Thousand Oaks, CA: Corwin Press, www.corwinpress.com. Reproduction authorized only for the local school site or nonprofit organization that has purchased this book.

Figure 5.1 (Continued)

My Personal Classroom Management Plan

Effective Teaching Practices

Building positive relationships

Between teacher and students

Among classmates

With parents

Strategies to develop student social skills

Strategies to develop student problem-solving and decision-making skills

Strategies to develop student self-control

Preventive discipline strategies

Classroom technology plan

Source: Copyright © 2006 by Corwin Press. All rights reserved. Reprinted from *Planning Classroom Management*, 2nd edition, by Karen Bosch. Thousand Oaks, CA: Corwin Press, www.corwinpress.com. Reproduction authorized only for the local school site or nonprofit organization that has purchased this book.

Figure 5.1 (Continued)

My Personal Classroom Management Plan

EVALUATION

Grading Scheme

Recording grades in the grade book

Homework policy

Progress reports

Student opportunities to impact their grades

Earning points

Extra credit

Rewrites

Drop a grade

Special assignments

Plan to factor the above opportunities into the student's final grade

Source: Copyright © 2006 by Corwin Press. All rights reserved. Reprinted from *Planning Classroom Management*, 2nd edition, by Karen Bosch. Thousand Oaks, CA: Corwin Press, www.corwinpress.com. Reproduction authorized only for the local school site or nonprofit organization that has purchased this book.

Figure 5.1 (Continued)

My Personal Classroom Management Plan

PROFESSIONAL DEVELOPMENT

Plans for improvement

Through reflective recall

Through journal writing

Through videotaping

Through mentorship

Through school inservices, college courses, and conferences

Source: Copyright © 2006 by Corwin Press. All rights reserved. Reprinted from *Planning Classroom Management*, 2nd edition, by Karen Bosch. Thousand Oaks, CA: Corwin Press, www.corwinpress.com. Reproduction authorized only for the local school site or nonprofit organization that has purchased this book.

One goal of the CMP is to engender a sense of community in the classroom, promoting and reinforcing positive actions and interactions so a cohesive, supportive group results. Classroom management is seen, heard, and felt in how a class gets along—how pleasant and respectful they are to each other (see Figure 5.2). This sense of community should extend beyond classroom walls to include parents. Classroom management is found in the relationship and developing trust between the teacher and his or her students, among classmates, and with parents. Marzano (2003) posits that an effective teacher–student relationship may be the keystone that allows other aspects of classroom management to work well (p. 91).

For teachers, students, and parents to be working partners, teachers must develop, nurture, and maintain a feeling of mutual respect, a positive rapport, and a cooperative spirit. Classroom management can't be autocratic, forced, coerced, or teacher directed; it must be democratic, desired, nurtured, and teacher–student centered. It is a participatory approach with teacher, students, and parents working together and sharing the responsibility to make the class work efficiently and effectively with positive outcomes—student success and teacher and learner satisfaction.

Draw or describe the room arrangement

Reflect on classroom seating arrangements and visualize the best arrangement to support teacher and student visibility and movement. As you describe the room arrangement, explain why this arrangement works for you. The key to classroom setup is flexibility: try not to get locked into any one arrangement. Furniture placement and seating arrangements should allow you and students to rearrange furniture easily to suit the activity, whether it involves students working independently, in pairs, or in groups.

The ability to maneuver in a room in the most efficient, quiet, and least obtrusive way is an objective for any classroom. Because many classrooms

Figure 5.2

Reflecting on Classroom Environment

- Write one word that best describes your classroom.

- How do you make sure this is the word everyone goes away with after visiting your classroom?

Remember that a perception or feeling or atmosphere isn't there just because you say so. It takes thought, reflection, planning, and effort. Ensure the perception of the class you desire by incorporating into your CMP the action to make it happen. For example, if you want your class to be inviting, what are you doing to make it inviting?

are crowded, teachers must spend time reflecting on the best arrangement. To plan the room arrangement, make a scale diagram first, and then place only furniture in the classroom that meets the teacher's and students' needs.

Sketch bulletin board ideas

Bulletin boards should be eye-catching and colorful. Use some bulletin board space for student work and teacher instructions. Let students know what's coming up both in class and in the school by posting announcements about such events as upcoming tests and school social events. If possible, make one board an interactive board relating to what students are working on. For example, while you're involved in individual instruction and have assigned seat work to the other students, they can go to the board for activities such as card games, worksheets, and so on. If you teach older students, one board should focus on current events. Post photos of people in the news and have students identify them for extra credit, or staple news clippings on the board, too, and have students match the photos with the news story. Put the class motto on the board (see Figure 5.3). Let students create a bulletin board and change it often to give them a role in how the classroom looks.

Classroom Operation

Day-to-day classroom operation is vital to classroom management. Teachers need to consider rules, routines and procedures, consequences, incentives, and cues.

Rules

Together, teacher and students should establish rules for the classroom that prohibit disrespectful behavior and set limits on disruptive behavior. Rules should be based on the principle that all students have a right to learn without such behavior infringing on it. The rules the class establishes provide structure to the classroom, and consistent enforcement and reinforcement of the rules is paramount. Teachers should be comfortable with the rules and able to enforce them.

Figure 5.3

Inspire Students With a Class Motto

Some examples of class mottos:

Attitude makes the difference!

Do your best to be your best!

Soar with the eagles or swim with the fish, just as long as you move toward your true potential!

"And so shines a good deed in a weary world."—Willy Wonka

Reach for the stars and become one!

Create relatively few rules so students have no trouble remembering them. Explain to them that rules in the classroom are very similar to society's rules: there is room for growth and individuality, and students have a lot of freedom until they impinge on other students' rights or the general learning atmosphere of the classroom.

As part of the democracy of the classroom, teachers must provide a means whereby students can suggest changes in the classroom operation, including the rules. This may be through a suggestion box, student polls or questionnaires, or a student advisory committee that helps teachers create and enforce classroom rules.

Routines and procedures

Think about what events take place daily (bell announcing start and end of class, beginning of lesson, taking attendance, journal writing, etc.) and decide what students are to do and how they are to behave at these times. For example, when the bell rings at the start of class, where should students be and what should they be doing? How do you give instructions so students have no question about the task and its objectives? What do students do when they finish an in-class activity? Are there routine tasks students might take over to give them responsibilities such as taking roll, distributing handouts, keeping time on group activities?

Think about implementing other procedures. For example, upon entering the classroom, students could write the day's learning objectives in their notebooks. Copying objectives provides students with a brief preview of the day's lessons. It is also a great organizing and study strategy: students can take notes and complete their assignments in their notebooks under the objectives. Or consider giving a math or word challenge, riddle, problem, or game students can work on until class starts and then discuss or solve it as a class.

Consequences

Teachers need to communicate their expectations regarding student behavior. Students should not have to guess at or "test" the consequences. Teachers should discuss consequences with students the first week of class and leave no doubt of the consequences for misbehavior. Once the class decides on rules and consequences, write them down and provide everyone, including parents, with a copy. A copy should also be on display in the classroom as a daily, physical reminder. Students can then choose their behavior with full understanding of the consequences, and, one hopes, they will choose discipline and self-control. Either way, they know the consequence they end up with was their choice. The use of rules and consequences teaches students that they are accountable for their actions and, as a result, it builds students' feelings of self-reliance and self-respect.

But meting out consequences can take a lot of class time—time better spent on instruction instead of correction. Teachers must ask themselves how much class time they take to enforce the consequences on a few students. If teachers find themselves spending too much time enforcing consequences, they must reflect on what to do differently.

It is important to remember that some students might interpret consequences and the time spent enforcing them as attention—negative attention, certainly, but attention nonetheless. Besides getting attention, repeated misbehavior may be a sign of a learning or emotional problem. If there seems to be a behavior problem, reflect more on the incentive side of the CMP—the buy-in to choosing good classroom behavior. Think about some preventive strategies such as establishing a better under-standing of and rapport with the student, holding a conference with the student and his or her parents, creating a written contract with the student for change, and, perhaps most importantly, allowing the student to offer solutions and both teacher and student making a commitment to follow these ideas.

If the problem stems from a learning difficulty, consult the learning resource teacher for techniques specific to student needs. For emotional problems, seek support from the resource personnel and school counselor.

Incentives

Individual and group incentives include grades, points, stickers, par-ties, free time, talk time, and homework passes. A teacher's verbal and nonverbal responses and students' responses to each other, both verbal and nonverbal, also serve as incentives. Nonverbal incentives include pats on the back, thumbs up, sports referee signals, sign language signals, nods, smiles, and winks.

Cues

Cues are facial expressions, body language, signals, codes, and voiced expressions that send messages, serve as reminders, offer encouragement and praise, reinforce activity, maintain effort, indicate the need for change, provide more direction, reduce distraction, discourage escalation of prob-lems, signal disapproval, serve as a reprimand, and give out punishment. Cues teach, enforce, and reinforce classroom management. Some examples of cues are sounding a whistle or bell, snapping the fingers or clapping the hands, and turning lights on and off.

INSTRUCTION

Classroom management supports teaching and student learning. Evertson et al. (1989) state that "the lesson outcomes you envision will determine your planning goals and objectives, and your plans should reflect these intended outcomes" (p. 117). Teachers plan lessons by first writing clear objectives. Taking this a step further, teachers with a clearly defined CMP create a learning environment that promotes the desired outcomes of both good instruction and good management.

Lessons

Teachers must ensure that lessons suit different learning styles, present lessons in an engaging manner, vary the presentation from lesson to lesson, state objectives clearly at the beginning of the lesson, and close the lesson by asking students to share what they have learned. Teachers who expect students to perform well and meet or exceed their potential provide stimulating lessons that teach students what they need to know and motivate them to want to learn more. Teachers can also inspire students by demonstrating enthusiasm and communicating by their demeanor that they enjoy teaching.

Instructional strategies

The various instructional strategies available to teachers are as numerous as the teachers themselves. Teachers should sample a variety of strategies, selecting those they feel most comfortable with and those that seem most effective. Teachers should remember, however, that all strategies require practice (see Figure 5.4). Many teachers attempting cooperative learning activities for the first time, for example, often feel they have lost control of the lesson when students work in groups—they have trouble selecting group members, have a hard time getting students to work productively, and they're unsure how to monitor the groups' progress. But trial and error is a part of cooperative learning activities. With practice, teachers can become comfortable with group activities by employing many management strategies such as assigning students to particular groups, offering incentives, and establishing rules for cooperative learning.

One direction-giving procedure that can facilitate cooperative learning activities or independent assignments begins with the "give and get" method, in which a teacher gives out specific and simple directions in steps and gets the instructions back by asking students what they are to do. Then the teacher sets a time limit and explains how he or she will collect and grade the assignment. Finally, the teacher asks if students have any questions. Students must understand this last step is the time to ask questions, not after the activity or assignment begins (Bosch, 1991).

Thematic, integrated units of study are an old but revived and exciting approach to teaching several different subjects together. An example of a theme could be a current event or a popular children's book, which might generate lessons that could conceivably cover language arts, social studies, science, math, art, music, character development, and computer technology.

Graphic organizers help students understand lessons, complete assignments, study for tests, and simply to organize their work. Examples of graphic organizers are Venn diagrams, KWL charts, bubble maps, and concept webs. Verbal advanced organizers are words that the teacher uses to prepare students for learning. Words such as first, next, last, finally, now, and later are a few of them and the list goes on.

Assessing students' prior knowledge is vital to the success of a lesson. Getting students to think about a subject by asking them what they already know about it primes them to receive additional information and make

Figure 5.4

Practice Makes Progress

Traditional classrooms have been mainly individual, independent, and competitive work environments, so interdependent, collaborative, and cooperative techniques need time and practice. Start cooperative learning activities by having students work in pairs, then move from pairs to groups of differing numbers. Try pair activities such as buddy read, dual practice, pair-role-project, pair-confer-report, and think-pair-share cooperative learning activities before moving to group activities such as team-accelerated instruction (TAI), student team achievement division (STAD), cooperative integrated reading and composition (CIRC), and Jigsaw I and II.

Don't dismiss an instructional strategy until you've tried it several times. Get feedback from students about what they like and dislike about the strategy. Remember, if you're using group work for the first time, your students may be just as uncomfortable with the process as you are. You may all need time to get used to a new idea and a new practice.

---

a connection between information they already possess and the new information. Previewing texts by asking students to look at chapter titles or subheadings is another way to prepare students to receive new information.

As often as possible, tie lessons into real life or conduct a simulation that mirrors real life. During presidential election years, many classrooms conduct their own elections. Using current events provides the relevant, meaningful connection that can breathe life into the required grade-level content and chosen curriculum or standards of learning that most school systems are mandating.

Review examinations after students take them. If everyone in the class missed one question, look closely at the question. Was it a bad question with confusing or tricky wording, or was it bad instruction that made them all miss it?

Success-building strategies are techniques teachers use to increase student participation, effort, and accomplishment. Examples include holding review sessions before each test to give students a chance to ask questions and to reinforce important aspects of the lessons; giving students an opportunity to respond to assignments in other ways beside writing, such as singing a song, performing a skit, or drawing a poster; initiating student contracts for learning differences, behavior improvement, and enrichment; asking higher-level questions that allow for more than one right answer; allowing students to collect points in classroom games and activities rather than "winning" and "losing"; and recognizing students for achievements other than "A" papers. See Figure 5.5 to reflect on instructional strategies.

Individualized instructional strategies

Teachers with classroom management skills are sensitive to the diverse needs of students in the classroom. Marzano (2003) states, "Effective classroom managers are aware of importance differences among students" (p. 101). Teachers must have a repertoire of specific strategies for meeting the special needs of learners in the classroom.

Figure 5.5

Reflecting on Instruction

- Provide some examples of encouragement you use.

- Record the direction-giving procedure you use each time you give directions to students.

- How do you ensure you give students adequate response time?

- How do you assess student learning?

- What procedure do students follow when they finish their work?

- List all the ways you select group participants for cooperative learning activities.

- What are your rules and responsibilities for working in groups?

- What are some ideas you have for great beginnings to lessons?

- What are some themes you use to teach integrated units of study?

- What graphic organizers do you use?

One individualized instructional strategy is to take an interest inventory: ask the student what kind of activities he or she enjoys. The answer gives the teacher an idea what kind of learner the student is—visual, oral, kinesthetic, and so on—then the teacher can structure activities so they build on the student's multiple intelligence strength and give alternative-style learners the opportunity to excel. Another strategy is giving a variety of options for evaluation. For example, for a writing exercise, give students the option of writing several shorter journal entries or one longer essay, performing a skit, or doing an interview, and let students choose the task that suits their strengths.

Contracts between teacher and student are particularly useful in cases of learning differences, behavior problems, and enrichment opportunities. A contract for learning differences is a program of study determined by teacher and student that may allow more time to complete assignments, fewer problems to complete at one time, different assignments from the rest of the class, and so on. Both the teacher and student sign, evaluate, and fulfill the terms of the contract. The behavioral contract is an agreement between the teacher and student that the student will change to more appropriate behavior. The contract is specific with shared expectations, incentives, and consequences for this effort. A contract for enrichment gives students opportunities to extend their learning, complete a project, write a report, draw a map, make a volcano, and so on. The strategies the teacher develops provide opportunities for the student to learn, progress, succeed, gain confidence, and take risks.

Assessing instructional strategies

Providing engaging instructional strategies is not enough to ensure all students have learned the material or have met with success. Assessing student learning must be done while the teacher is teaching, and again when the student is practicing the new information. Guided practice activities are opportunities for students to practice and learn the information that was taught to them in the lesson. Some strategies for teachers to use in assessing the student learning of new information are the following:

- Watch student body language (i.e., squinting eyes, limited or no eye contact, head resting on hand or desk).
- Monitor the level of learner interest and involvement (i.e., few hands raised; few comments made; reduced level of participation by diverse populations of learners, special needs students, etc.).
- Use a student accountability cue or signal such as a "thumbs up," "thumbs sideways," or "thumbs down" to indicate the students' level of understanding of the concept, question, assignment, or directions. The teacher can ask a question such as, "How many agree with this statement?" Some students may be looking around at others before raising their hands or some may be raising their hands half way, and so forth. The teacher needs to observe the students when using the cuing signals and then act on the information received or the behavior

shown. If necessary, provide more information or examples, ask more questions, or assign more guided practice to have students indicate a better understanding.

- Interject a quick-scan idea by having students use individual white boards to write their answers and raise them all at one time for teacher to note the students' answers. Small personal chalkboards or a transparency on individual clipboards can be used for this quick scan. Teachers can also use note cards that have "Yes," "Maybe," or "No" written on them and students can raise one.

Questioning strategies

Questioning is a skill teachers must develop and practice to improve student learning. Questions should enable students to apply prior knowledge and experience to the new knowledge being acquired, to enhance learning of the material. Becoming more familiar with and more skillful in using Bloom's (1956) Taxonomy of Cognitive Domains creates a learning environment for all learners. The taxonomy is a structure, but within any structure there is flexibility, spontaneity, and the ability to move from one area to the next and not always in order. Questions can move within the taxonomy for improved student learning.

Examples of questions

When asking questions from Bloom's (1956) Taxonomy, take a minute to reflect on the value it has for all learners to experience all levels of thinking. More importantly, be aware of the need as a teacher to reach into the areas of analysis, synthesis, and evaluation with questions. In reviewing the taxonomy, such questions begin with asking students to demonstrate knowledge (recall) and comprehension (interpretation), then to use application (apply), analysis (break apart), synthesis (put together), and evaluation (judge). Usually, the first two or three domains are covered by the teacher in asking questions; however, the following three areas—analysis, synthesis, and evaluation—are often overlooked. Embedded in the last three areas, we find that more motivation is found and an increased level of participation by all learners. Questioning learners from the last three areas provides an environment that is label-free, risk-free, and can equalize the playing field. Think of responding to a question that is asking your opinion and it has no right or wrong, yes or no, or one-way thinking answer. What could contribute more to the learning potential, confidence, and success of all learners? If the subject is the fairy tale *Cinderella*, ask students if they can remember a time when they felt like the main character—an application question. Under analysis, have students determine three of the main character's qualities. Then based on synthesis, ask from what they know of the character, how might the character behave if placed in their town? Under evaluation, ask if they were the main character, would they have taken the same action? Do they think the character did the right thing?

Responses to students

Determine ahead of time how you will react to students when they give a correct answer, a partially correct answer, or an incorrect answer. Your response should demonstrate respect for their attempts and encouragement to try again. For example, if the answer is partially correct, you might say, "Your answer is a good start, but let's add some more information." If, however, the subject is math or another subject where the answer is either right or wrong and the student answers incorrectly, you might say, "Let's see how you got that answer."

Student self-evaluation opportunities

Self-evaluation is a way for students to monitor their learning and an opportunity for teachers to foster more student autonomy. Through self-evaluation, students can determine grades, progress, improvement, strengths, areas of weakness, missing assignments, mastery of skills, and skills needing practice. The student spends time observing and collecting information pertaining to these areas. For example, students might make a graph to record their grades on in-class assignments, tests, quizzes, and homework. The graph provides a visual self-evaluation of progress.

Effective Teaching Practices

Effective teaching practices are behaviors that promote learning and create a positive classroom atmosphere (see Figure 5.6). Offering praise and encouragement, providing feedback, and communicating high expectations are specific ways teachers can help create a positive classroom atmosphere. Brophy (1981) reminds teachers that praise has an active role in any classroom. Praise feels good—everyone wants to receive it—and it is an incentive for most. Praise projects approval, agreement, acknowledgment, support, and satisfaction. Praise is expressed in such expressions as "Great effort!" "Super worker!" "Wow! I like that!" "Good detail, nice work!" "Exactly!" "Interesting!" "Creative!" "You are prepared!" "I like your thinking!" "Your thinking cap is on today!" Some examples of encouragement are "You are on a roll!" "I know you are thinking about that topic sentence!" "Good start!" "Keep it up!" "Terrific beginning, can't wait to read the rest!"

Teachers can offer feedback in the form of oral and written comments and suggestions during guided practice and question-and-answer sessions, as well as on homework, in-class assignments, progress reports, and notes home to parents. Feedback must be specific and clear and must provide the student with the opportunity to act on it. Some examples of feedback statements are, "This is good. If you add an example it will be extraordinary!" "Good start on that description of the main character! Can you add two more adjectives?" "You have compared the two characters, now add some contrast." Written feedback on papers offers so much more to a learner than comments such as "Vague," "Awkward," and "Do over!" Written feedback includes, "Every paragraph needs at least three details,"

Figure 5.6

Supportive Strategies

- Provide some examples of how you demonstrate high expectations for student learning.

- Provide an example of how you use the positive ripple effect.

- How do you develop a sense of group cohesiveness, class camaraderie, and community?

- How do you help students get involved in community projects?

- What opportunities do you give your students to change how the classroom works?

- How do you conduct classroom meetings?

- What is your strategy to ensure all students in class participate?

"Remember to indent when you discuss each new idea," "Research papers need at least five sources, and remember to cite references in the text." Feedback provides information the learner can act upon to learn.

One way of treating students with dignity and respect is to expect them to do well. High expectations are important to student achievement. Teacher statements and actions can demonstrate this confidence in students or undermine students' efforts. For example, a teacher can demonstrate high expectations by saying, "I know you can do this assignment well," or defeat such expectations by saying, "This is a difficult assignment, probably too hard for most."

Building positive relationships

Relationship-building strategies are vital to the CMP development. Teachers need to build personal relationships with students by building into the CMP get-acquainted activities; getting-to-know-you exercises; interest surveys; teacher–student conferences; class discussions; and opportunities for student involvement, input, and self-control. A study conducted by Brown (2004) discusses several management strategies that reflect culturally responsive teaching such as developing personal relationships with students, creating caring communities, establishing businesslike learning environments, and clearly stating and enforcing expectations.

Teachers also need to provide in the CMP many ways to create, encourage, and reward positive classmate relationships through such ideas as a buddy system, group activities and projects, peer tutoring, and "catch them being good to each other" incentives. Teachers can build into the CMP ways to work with parents such as an introductory letter; making positive phone calls before asking for support; soliciting their help with class activities and needs; keeping them informed by sending papers home once a week; sending home a student-created newsletter; alerting parents early before problems escalate or grades drop; and being accessible to parents by means of phone, e-mail, and posted office hours.

Between teacher and students: Teacher–student conferences, for example, to discuss progress, grades, discipline, or any other topic are a powerful and meaningful strategy to build relationships. Conferences between the teacher and the student open the lines of communication, establish rapport, and help develop respect for each other. A teacher and student can develop a plan of action—a contract or agreement—to work through areas of special needs or behavioral concerns.

Students feel more empowered when it comes to evaluation, and they feel they have more input and control in how the class operates. Holding class meetings on a regular basis in which teachers discuss with students everything that goes on in the classroom, from lessons to student behavior to decorations, is another valuable way to build relationships. Class meetings also create and maintain a sense of ownership among classmates for the classroom and the way it operates.

Among classmates: Positive student relationships are important to how the class works. Teachers can foster these relationships by giving students many opportunities to work together. Allow students time to get to know each other. Peer tutoring, peer assistance, and even the buddy system are opportunities for students to learn how to work together and learn together. Class activities can bring the group together such as working together on a community or school project; creating a bulletin board; planning school functions; or participating in fairs, a class open house, and science night.

With parents: Keep parents informed about what goes on in the classroom. Send a letter to them at the beginning of the year, making them aware of your goals for the year, and send another letter at the end of the year telling them how much you enjoyed working with their child. Send home letters announcing upcoming units, perhaps asking for parents with expertise in that area to visit the classroom. Keep your door open to parents. Make sure they feel welcomed in your classroom. To reinforce the community spirit, include students in parent conferences, if appropriate. Send home a copy of your classroom rules and consequences as well. A student, teacher, and parent create a learning triad—a team that can work together for school success.

Strategies to develop student social skills

Teachers may need to teach, review, and reinforce social skills and establish rules of conduct and rules for communicating when students work together. Include classroom texts that contain some social skill emphasis, make assignments that employ social skills and discuss why they are important, and share experiences requiring social skills.

Students need opportunities to practice social skills. Include time in the day for nonacademic discussion to get students to interact in a more social way. Develop scenarios and have students role-play, read books for discussion on social issues and behaviors, or establish a list of positive ways to communicate with one another. Create strategies and procedures to assist the class in using social skills. For example, remind students that they are to respect each other at all times, even when they disagree. When introducing think-pair-share activities to them for the first time, tell students the primary rule is that they must be accepting of others' ideas.

Strategies to develop student problem-solving and decision-making skills

Problem-solving and decision-making strategies support learners in times of doubt, confusion, and frustration, and when they have questions or need assistance. For example, one strategy to help students become problem solvers is the Unstuck Procedure, which helps a learner having a problem with an assignment: Students should first, reread the directions; second, go on to the next problem; third, ask a peer for help; fourth, place a colored index card on the desk to indicate the need for teacher assistance; and, finally, take out other work to do or a library book to read silently until the teacher can help (Bosch & Kersey, 2000, pp. 88–89).

Have the class decide on problem-solving procedures; for example, to resolve the problem of what to do when they have finished their work, the class may decide to choose from the following options: place a Finished card (a colored index card) on the corner of the desk, start other class assignments, read a library book, go to the learning center, or use the computer.

Strategies to develop student self-control

Students who have difficulty with self-control need to practice self-management techniques. The teacher and the student may decide to create a monitoring plan. For example, the student focuses on one behavior and the teacher and student thoroughly discuss what the student needs to do to practice a more appropriate behavior. The student places an index card listing that behavior on his or her desk. The student records with an X the number of times he or she demonstrates this behavior in a day for each day of the week. At the end of the day or week, the teacher and student discuss the student's progress. The student can count and see the Xs on the card that show progress. The teacher can also have the student graph the Xs, then by reflecting on the collected data, the student and teacher can see trends and draw conclusions. When the graph continually improves and the number of Xs continues to increase, practice another behavior.

In many classrooms, students go voluntarily to a time-out place to regain composure for an amount of time decided by the teacher or the class. When the amount of time has been served, the student returns to his or her seat. The class can also decide on ways to solve conflicts. For example, if two students are arguing, the class may ask the designated "class lawyer" to listen to the problem. If a classmate fights physically with another classmate, the resolution plan may be to place chairs back to back and have students each take a seat. Each student must tell the class the problem. Next, each student tells how the problem started and how the problem can end. Then, the two students need to decide and tell the class how they will work together to solve the problem. In other conflict resolution plans, a forum to air problems may be found in class meetings or in convening a class court.

Preventive discipline strategies

Preventing discipline problems requires an attentive and responsive teacher who is alert to students, their needs, and ever-changing classroom conditions. Teachers must determine what kind of behavior they will ignore and how they will exhibit disapproval to students who misbehave (see Figure 5.7). Body language is quick, effective, and powerful: eye contact and proximity may be all that is necessary to stop inappropriate behavior.

Figure 5.7

Reflecting on Discipline Strategies

- What is the first level of disapproval you will demonstrate to the student?

- What kind of behavior will you ignore?

- How will you use eye contact and proximity to stop inappropriate behavior?

Classroom technology plan

The first step in creating a classroom technology plan is determining what resources are available in the classroom. For example, does your room have a television, VCR or DVD player, tape recorder, or computers? Next, specifically describe how you use technology in the teaching and learning of lessons, and how you use the classroom computer(s) and the school's computer lab.

The use of media, visual aids, and resources shows teacher planning and preparation. Students and others view the use of such resources as extra effort by teachers (see also Figure 5.8). If the teacher is viewed as having done his or her homework, trying hard to do more not less, and attempting to do the best job possible, this becomes a class norm, value, and expectation. The teacher is modeling a behavior that can be expected from students.

Figure 5.8

Be "Resource" full

Are art supplies accessible, or do you have to order them from another location in the school? Do you have globes, maps, and a set of encyclopedias? What about human resources: Do you have aides? Do you team teach? Do you have parents or other volunteers who help out in the classroom?

Think about the classroom resources available in addition to electronic resources. Teachers find that reflecting on the curriculum and its objectives and even some lessons helps them plan better use of resources. The teacher can collect information; search for the information on the Internet; collect supplies from the media room or center; order in advance the tapes, pictures, and materials for the lessons; purchase materials; get related books from the library; plan time with the librarian for use of the library; and sign up for the computer lab. The teacher can ask for resources from other teachers and solicit information and support from parents. Parents can also be a resource. Teaching with resources can spark interest and enthusiasm for learning, make content clearer, activate students' prior knowledge, and help meet individual needs for learning based on multiple intelligences and learning styles theories.

EVALUATION

The evaluative structure of classroom management must have a two-way communication flow. Too often, students report that grades are what a teacher gives to them. Students should feel they have *earned* their grades. Grades are earned when the person being graded is given feedback, has some input, and has been afforded opportunities to impact the grade or how the evaluation is conducted. This feeling of empowerment is necessary in gaining students' full participation and commitment to learn, continue learning, and improve their learning.

When evaluating students, be sure their work matches the objective of the lesson. Simply put, if you told them to sing a song, they can't dance a dance. Some teachers find creating a contract with students is an effective way of giving them input in their grade as well as giving alternative-style learners an assessment option. The contract makes goals and objectives for a unit of study explicit; for example, "This is the reading unit, and this is what you must accomplish during this unit." Have students sign the written contract. If they don't accomplish the terms of the contract, their grade reflects it.

Grading Scheme

Your grading scheme represents what you believe about students, teaching, and learning (refer back to the Reflection Questionnaire in Chapter 3). The plan should be fair and reflect curriculum standards yet be flexible and provide opportunities for students to improve grades. The plan must be one you can and want to support and consistently apply to classroom assignments and tests. For the CMP to provide consistency, your grading scheme must support the ideas set forth in the Reflection Questionnaire and in the CMP.

Recording grades in the grade book

Consider how you will manage the grade book if assignments count for different percentages or you allow students to redo certain assignments in an attempt to improve their grade. How will you note the first grade, then the second? The record of this must be clear and orderly in the grade book. If quizzes count for a certain percentage and tests another percentage, the grade book must display the difference for ease in final calculation of the grade. Most importantly, students must be allowed to see their grades to monitor their progress. A grade book can paint a picture of a student's effort, ability, proficiency, reliability, and attitude. Grades should not be a secret or a mystery to learners.

Homework policy

For homework to be important and for students to do it, it must have some impact on the final grade for the grading period. Develop a homework policy and teach it. As you write the CMP, consider the following: How much does homework count in the evaluation plan? When and how is it collected? When is it considered late? If students have done it but forgotten it, when is the latest time to get it in and still receive credit? How many days do students get to complete homework when absent? Homework that is partnered with a policy and an incentive—the incentive being that it has an effect on their grade—fosters more student involvement, commitment, effort, and practice time for learning.

Progress reports

Progress reports give students feedback and allow them to evaluate their progress or lack of it and make decisions about changing the course of events. Grades, progress, or lack of progress should not be a surprise to the learner. Learners need to know their status and get feedback on how to do better or what to do differently. If students are to be more responsible and accountable for their own learning, teachers must provide an opportunity for them to take and accept more control. Progress reports could do just that, if planned as a student opportunity to affect their grade.

Student opportunities to impact grades

Students must be able to exercise some control over their learning and their grades. Effort should play a greater role in their work for effort equals outcome. Students must have opportunities to affect their grades through such avenues as extra credit, rewrites, dropping a grade, special assignments, and collection of points for cooperative learning activities and independent tasks. These opportunities offer students options and possibilities, then leave it to students to take advantage of them and take charge of their own learning.

PROFESSIONAL DEVELOPMENT

The final step in writing a personal CMP is reflecting on your classroom management and teaching for professional growth and development. In this section of the CMP, the goal is to provide ways for you to reflect not only on each school day but the year as well. Roberts, Kellough, and Moore (2006) suggest that reflecting on one's teaching is inevitable but professional growth is not as inevitable unless it is self-initiated and systematically planned (p. 282).

Through Reflection

Reflection may be a critique of a teaching lesson, learning activity, classroom situation, or behavioral problem. The evaluative aspects of reflection provide teachers with an opportunity to get in touch with their teaching selves, analyze their teaching goals, and chart a new course of action in achieving their goals. Kohn (1996) suggests that teachers be "encouraged to think about their long-term goals and about whether their classrooms are really animated by these goals" (p. 68).

This thinking about one's teaching can be a personal or a peer reflective process. It can be taken to another level by including the expertise of the building principal, assistant principal, or district office supervisors. Some teachers may want to observe other teachers or have others observe their teaching. Others may want to share teaching experiences with their college professors and jointly discuss possible changes.

Through Reflective Recall

Reflective recall is a method that lets teachers use time, thought, and insight to impact how they and the classroom work. Reflective recall has a three-step approach: Stop, Recall, and Review.

In the first step, teachers must physically stop everything to spend time reflecting on a lesson, situation, problem, or concern. It is necessary for teachers to allot time routinely to stop the busyness of teaching and just think about their class, their teaching, and their students' learning. Teachers must also schedule a place to do this reflective thinking. Perhaps a teacher can find a comfortable place to work that is bright and cheerful; possibly a corner of the room with a window. This place definitely needs to be out of the mainstream, away from phones and interruptions.

The next step is to recall lessons, events, situations, and experiences. Once stopped, teachers can begin to think about the day, morning, or afternoon; or a unit of study, lesson, or objective or two, including their students' learning; and everyone's effectiveness, willingness, and productivity. Teachers should focus solely on that recalled information.

In the review step, teachers think about the recalled information and connect the information to the CMP. A teacher can focus on a particular problem—such as too little productivity when working in cooperative groups. The teacher reflects on the information and asks, What can I do to change this behavior? The teacher asks such questions as, Why aren't the students accomplishing more when working in groups? Is the assignment specific? Do they have enough time? Do I need more management strategies operating in my groups such as assigning roles like leader, recorder, time manager, and noise monitor? Do I need to provide incentives to raise the level of work quality? The teacher may want to write down the ideas and begin implementing some of them on the next class day.

The Stop, Recall, Review process is an important part of the practice of teaching. To be and remain effective, teachers need to evaluate their own as well as students' classroom performance and behavior, recalling how they work and how the classroom works.

Through Journal Writing

Another way for teachers to grow professionally is to maintain a journal. The journal entries record the process of reflective thinking and learning. The teacher can write down concerns and questions and discuss possible solutions. This way, the journal can document your problem-solving and decision-making processes.

Through Videotaping

Videotaping provides an opportunity for the teacher to view his or her teaching performance individually, or possibly with another teacher or mentor. The videotape is a visual account of teaching a lesson or it can document parts of a school day that show the teacher at work. Herein lies another opportunity for professional growth and development that may lead to change and improved performance (see Figure 5.9).

Through Mentorship

In many schools, a first-year teacher is assigned a mentor. The mentor is an experienced, practicing teacher who becomes a listener, supporter, coach, and confidante to another, less experienced teacher. The mentor can meet with the teacher at designated times and discuss areas of concern. He or she can observe the teacher and provide feedback for improvement. Little (1990) maintains that mentoring arrangements may be a way to reform teaching and retain teachers in the profession. The teacher can establish mentoring relationships with others in the school or school system, such as a peer teacher, grade-level chairperson, principals, and district supervisors, and from professionals outside of the school systems, such as college professors.

Through School Inservices, College Courses, and Conferences

Inservice activities that are sponsored by the school or school system continue the professional development of practicing teachers. Inservice opportunities can introduce teachers to current management and teaching skills and update old skills. The teacher can continue to learn about teaching by taking college courses. College courses provide a more in-depth approach to improving teaching skills. Attending workshops and conferences provides yet another opportunity to update and improve a teacher's knowledge and skills. A teacher must always remain a student of his or her profession.

Reflection requires thought, self-direction, and problem solving (Elliott, 1991). Teachers must train themselves to concentrate on and critique their teaching, classroom management, and student learning. A teacher can recall lessons, situations, problems, or concerns from memory, from notes taken during observations, and from videotapes of lessons and activities.

Students can also help teachers observe and reflect. Teachers should take the time to find out what students like and what they think works. Ask them which units they found most interesting and which were least interesting. Have them respond to a questionnaire with content such as "I feel

Figure 5.9

Reflecting Through Videotape

Teachers can make a videotape of a lesson or activity and apply the same reflective recall method in working with the videotape.

- Stop the tape at different places.

- Recall what is happening.

- Review areas of the CMP pertaining to the situation on screen.

Make plans to incorporate these new ideas into a CMP mini-lesson taught to students (see Chapter 6).

---

good when Mr. Smith _____," or "I feel bad when _____ happens in class." At the end of the term or year, give them a list of the units covered during the period, and ask them to rank them according to which interested them most. Then ask them why they liked some units and not others. These methods of reflection in conjunction with a review of the CMP may lead to constructive revising and refinement of the CMP.

For Further Study

- Complete this statement in as many ways as you can: Reflective teachers are . . .
- Take a lesson that didn't go well. A good starting point is to create a reflection web with the concern or problem in the center. Draw lines radiating from the center and on the lines write possible solutions. Use the web to explore ways to change and improve the situation.

6

Implementing the Classroom Management Plan

After their conversation in the teacher's lounge, Jennifer and Kate began meeting each week over coffee to discuss their classes. Tonight, at Jennifer's request, Kate had brought her classroom management plan and a folder full of lesson plans.

"I always thought of classroom management as an idea—you know, an abstract concept," Jennifer said as she looked over the materials Kate had brought. "I never thought about writing a plan for it, making it something tangible."

"I felt the same way," Kate admitted. "In fact, when I first started teaching, I felt a little lost. I knew my subject matter, I liked the kids, but I had trouble managing my classroom time. I would make my lesson plan but never get through it before class ended. There'd be distractions and interruptions, I'd spend far too much time repeating instructions for assignments, or I'd assign seat work so I could meet with students individually, and my students would end up chatting about the upcoming dance or making paper airplanes out of my worksheets.

"Every year, students voted Anne Cooper the Teacher of the Year. And Anne taught math, for heaven's sake! When students vote a math teacher the best of the year, you know she's doing something special. So I asked her if I could sit in on her class. And I was amazed. Her students worked hard, but they seemed to be having a good time, too. I couldn't really put my finger on what she was doing or how, but the atmosphere in her classroom was charged. I met with her after my visit, and she showed me her classroom management plan. Then I went home and wrote one up right then and there."

"Do you mind if borrow your plan and these lesson plans for a little while?" Jennifer asked. "I'd like to take some time to look them over. I know I can get some good ideas from them."

"Take your time with them," Kate answered.

"But I don't think I could do all of this." Jennifer looked uncomfortable for a moment. "Do you really dress up as characters in history when you teach?"

Kate laughed. "I do, yes. But that doesn't mean you have to. Take from my plan and my lessons anything you can use, but don't expect to borrow from them wholesale. Borrow a little or borrow a lot, but adapt them so your plan and your lessons suit your teaching style and your personality."

"I will!" Jennifer exclaimed with a grin. "I feel like I'm a new teacher again! And I think my students are in for a surprise."

SET THE CMP IN MOTION

Implementation is the fourth step of the classroom management process. The CMP is now a relevant, comprehensive, and integrative plan to build classroom management into how a teacher works and how a classroom works.

Teaching students the rules, routines and procedures, consequences, and incentives of the classroom begins the implementation of the CMP. Teachers can teach their CMP along with the curriculum by planning CMP mini-lessons. Depending on whether the lesson is to teach or review the components of the CMP, the lessons may take as long as 30 minutes or as little as 10 minutes. Teachers can intersperse the CMP mini-lessons throughout the school day as needed to teach, review, or reinforce areas of the CMP. These CMP lessons are just as important as curriculum objectives, lessons, and goals.

Teachers may express concern about the time required to plan CMP lessons, but planning the mini-lessons can be done in advance of the school year. Preservice teachers can develop mini-lessons in teacher education courses and during their field experiences. Inservice workshops for practicing teachers can provide a planning session for the writing of CMP mini-lessons. Both preservice and practicing teachers can develop the lessons alone or in groups and exchange them with peers. The lessons can be collected and placed in a notebook in the school library and used by all teachers.

Teachers have stated that they have no time in the day to teach additional lessons, that curriculum fills the school hours. Herein lies the commitment teachers must make to their profession. Building classroom management into each school day begins with preparing and teaching the CMP. Preparing the CMP can begin before the first day of school; however, *teaching* the CMP must begin the first day of school. Bosch and Kersey (2000) have developed an effective classroom management plan for the first four weeks of class to assist first-year teachers in becoming effective managers. Evertson (1989) stresses that "solving managerial and organizational problems at the beginning of the year is essential in laying the groundwork for quality learning experiences for students" (p. 90). Wong and Wong (1998) maintain that good control of the class needs to be established in the first week of school. Good control does not mean threats and intimidation but simply knowing what one is doing.

PLANNING CMP MINI-LESSONS

Teachers need to think seriously about the teaching and learning that take place in the first few weeks of each school year. Much time is spent in review; specifically, teachers try to determine what students know and can apply to the learning of new skills. Streamlining the review that begins every school year not only creates time for teaching the CMP, but it can also reduce the boredom, downtime, and segregation of learners based on interest, ability, and aptitude.

The CMP implemented with commitment continually supports more student learning and the rigors of the curriculum. The CMP taught and learned affirms within the teacher and students a sense of pride and ownership for how "their" class works. The CMP ensures a level of teacher and student autonomy, competence, confidence, interdependence, and accountability that is needed in today's classrooms.

The number of CMP mini-lessons and the amount of time allotted to teaching each lesson depend on the teacher and the class. Teachers must make decisions based on how they teach the CMP and its components and observing whether students have learned the information. But the CMP should begin to operate on the first day and continue until the last day of the school year.

Effective Lesson Structure

Like all good lessons, the sample CMP mini-lessons in this chapter have the following four necessary elements: objectives, opener, instruction, and closure (see Figure 6.1). A list of materials needed and an independent practice activity may also be included for each lesson.

Objectives

The lesson plan begins with the objectives. Teachers need to communicate the reasons for teaching the lesson to students, and students must understand what they are expected to learn in the amount of time of the lesson. Knowing their respective responsibilities for the teaching and learning of the lesson material during the block of time can also keep teacher and students on task. To this end, write the lesson objectives on the board or overhead.

Opener

The second element is the opener. The opener is the first impression, the hook that gets students' attention. It must be interesting, relevant, and engaging. The opener can be a cartoon, story, quote, picture, role-play, or

Figure 6.1

CMP Mini-Lesson

Grade:
Time:
Materials:

Objectives:

Opener:

Instruction:

Closure:

Independent Practice:

Source: Copyright © 2006 by Corwin Press. All rights reserved. Reprinted from *Planning Classroom Management*, 2nd edition, by Karen Bosch. Thousand Oaks, CA: Corwin Press, www.corwinpress.com. Reproduction authorized only for the local school site or nonprofit organization that has purchased this book.

something similar. The opener lasts approximately two to three minutes, five at maximum, and facilitates a smooth transition into instruction.

Instruction

The next element of the lesson is instruction. Teachers need to plan instruction to include both a teaching strategy and a learning strategy for each objective of the lesson. A teaching strategy is how the teacher teaches the lesson and a learning strategy is how the learner will learn, or practice, the lesson. Keeping these two areas distinct in the lesson plan enables the teacher to move from the role of instructor to that of facilitator. After the lesson, while students are trying out or practicing their understanding of the new information, the teacher becomes a facilitator, circulating around the room helping students and assessing their understanding.

Assessing students' learning includes observing their willingness to participate, their level of decisiveness in responding, any hesitation in starting the assignment, and their difficulty with the assignment. Assessing requires teacher alertness and attentiveness to the learning needs of students. It consists of the teacher making eye contact, scanning the room frequently, moving around the room, and noticing student difficulties (see also Figure 6.2). Teachers need to plan assessing moments or activities in their lessons during which they observe and assess student learning. Assessing student learning renders results only if teachers plan for it, collect information, and then apply this information to their teaching.

If, during assessment activities, the teacher observes students having difficulty learning the information, he or she can decide to return to teaching and provide more examples, offer more guided practice, or change the teaching/learning exchange.

Three teaching/learning exchanges exist: 1. teacher to students, or direct classroom instruction; 2. student to student, or grouping situations; and 3. one-on-one, or individualized instruction. When students experience difficulty, teachers must consider changing the teaching/learning exchange. For example, if students do not understand the material through the first exchange—direct teaching as in a lecture—teachers should try the second level of exchange, which is student to student, students learning from each other in a group, or cooperative, collaborative setting. This gives students a chance to learn from their peers. If that level doesn't work, teachers can try the third level, which is one-on-one teaching, or individualized instruction. This is a tutorial relationship between a tutor and the tutee primarily used for teaching, reviewing, and reteaching material.

In addition to assessing student learning during the teaching of the lesson, the teacher must ascertain the student learning quotient (LQ)—the number of students who understand the material divided by the total number of students in the class. Then convert this number to a percentage. This percentage gives the teacher a sense of what the majority knows. If the majority of students understand the material, the teacher can and must move on, making sure to note who *doesn't* understand so as to help them independently. If less than the majority understands, the teacher should

Figure 6.2

> **Signs of Uncertainty**
>
> Students who don't understand the lesson, information, or directions or who are experiencing difficulty in the guided practice activity unconsciously move their necks forward and squint their eyes in a manner one can call the "learning jerk." Teachers need to monitor students during instruction to recognize the messages they send about their learning. The learning jerk is a telltale sign of individuals needing more instruction or practice learning the information.

continue teaching that part of the lesson by sharing more content, asking more questions, providing more examples, changing the teaching/learning exchange, or offering additional guided practice activities.

To determine the student LQ, teachers seek answers to the following three questions during the guided practice activity: Who knows, who *doesn't* know, and *how many* know the information. Thus, to collect the LQ, teachers teach to the first objective, assign a guided practice activity, then monitor and assess students' learning. To assess the LQ, teachers might do the following: Give students a problem and two answers to choose from. Ask for a show of hands on those who choose answer #1 and another for those who select answer #2. This exercise indicates quickly who knows the answer. Teachers can also walk around and check students' work, or practice "clipboarding," which is a strategy where a teacher uses a copy of the student roll on which the lesson's objectives are listed. With the roll in hand, teachers can monitor a guided practice activity and record the LQ by placing codes next to students' names: + = mastery of the information, O = acceptable understanding, and – = marginal understanding. This information can help teachers teach the current lesson plan, make more appropriate assignments, select group members for cooperative learning activities, and provide individual attention time or peer tutoring for some students. In addition, recording LQ information may help teachers in the reflection process. The LQ information can reveal areas for teachers to reflect on for improved lesson planning and to increase all students' learning.

Closure

The final element in a lesson is closure. An appropriately planned closure allows students to express *what* they have learned and to realize that they, indeed, *have* learned something. During the closure portion of the lesson, the teacher listens for what has been taught coming back in student words. Closure can provide learners with confidence that they've achieved the lesson objectives. It also brings purpose to learning. Students who do not take an active part in the closure of the lesson probably don't know what they know or have learned. This may be one reason, when asked by teachers or parents what they did in school today, students frequently respond by saying, "Nothing." Or when asked, "How was school?" they say "Boring"—they haven't been taught to give back information.

They haven't had the chance to think through their learning. Closure is that chance.

Elementary school teachers should try to provide closure at the end of the day for all activities as well as for each lesson. They should ask students what they learned today, or what they can't wait to tell their parent about school, or what is one thing they think they could teach their brother or sister that they learned today. Then when asked what they did in school that day, students will have something to say because they have had a chance to organize and think about their learning. Their answer will undoubtedly generate a positive response from their questioner, which will make them feel good about themselves and want to learn more.

The Power of Learning

When teachers highlight the objectives for the lesson, plan an inviting opener, teach the CMP mini-lesson, assess student learning during instruction, and provide more student-generated closures, students can be more autonomous, accountable, and empowered in their learning. As Glasser (1986) states, "A good school could be defined as a place where almost all students believe that if they do some work, they will be able to satisfy their needs enough so that it makes sense to keep working" (p. 15). Creating independent learners is one of the goals of schooling. The CMP provides the structure for students to practice autonomy in the classroom and in their learning and be part of a community of learners. Teachers cannot expect students to be independent learners without providing them with opportunities to learn to be more independent and feel the empowerment of knowledge.

TEACHING THE CMP

The discussions and mini-lesson plans in this chapter have been developed to assist in teaching the CMP to the class. The lessons are designed for a variety of grade levels and require differing amounts of teaching time. CMP mini-lessons may have to be taught more than once to the class, or shorter but more precise classroom management mini-lessons may be needed for review and reinforcement of the plan's components. Teachers must not assume that if they teach a component of the CMP once, students will understand and follow it. CMP objectives need the same commitment to learning frequently brought to curriculum objectives such as review, practice, and reinforcement. Teachers must teach a CMP mini-lesson, then assess whether students have learned the lesson and achieved the objectives. If students do not follow the information, teachers must reteach, review, and reinforce the lesson and constantly convey higher expectations for learning the information. Consistent use and reinforcement of the CMP sends a strong and clear message that this is how the class works.

Introduce the CMP Early

Teachers need to introduce the CMP to students on the first day of class, for this is the time students must begin to understand the way teachers plan to work and how they plan to have the classroom work. Teachers can teach the need for and importance of a CMP with Sample Mini-Lesson 1 (see below) and also use this lesson plan to create, develop, and even review one or more components of the CMP.

SAMPLE MINI-LESSON 1

CMP MINI-LESSON FOR INTRODUCING THE CMP AND ITS COMPONENTS

Grade Level: 1–12

Time: 10–30 minutes

Objectives

Students will be able to

- recognize the need for and importance of a CMP or a component of the CMP.

- develop a component or strategy for the CMP.

- apply the CMP and its components to several classroom situations.

Opener

Ask students if the following quotes sound familiar:

"I'm finished with my work; what do I do now?"

"What is the homework policy?"

"What happens if I'm sick?"

"How will you grade this?"

Discuss the sentence, "I love it when a plan comes together!" Focus on such terms as plans, procedures, and policies. Tell them this class will have a classroom management plan, or CMP. Together, the class will develop a CMP that structures how the class will work.

Instruction

Ask students to brainstorm about why a classroom plan is important to both the teacher and students. Place their ideas on the chalkboard or overhead.

Define the CMP as a plan to structure a secure, organized, effective learning environment conducive to meeting the needs of students throughout the day, class, or course.

Explain to students briefly that a CMP is a plan with components, or parts. Discuss the role you want students to have in creating or developing the components. Explain, for example, that students can create a component of the CMP such as a problem-solving strategy. Ask students why problem-solving strategies are important, and ask them to name some classroom problems. What, for example, was the first problem mentioned in the opener? Place student suggestions on the board for "I'm finished with my work; what do I do now?" Place students into groups and have them write scenarios that require problem-solving strategies. Then have them share their scenarios and create problem-solving strategies to solve these problems.

Variation 1

Place students into groups of four and give them an index card on which is written a scenario of a problem. Each card has a different scenario; for example, one card may read, "John has been out of school for four days. He has a lot of work to make up. How can John get his work done?"

What kind of homework makeup policy should the class have? How can the class support John in getting his work done? Have students brainstorm, then share their scenarios and suggestions for the homework policy.

Variation 2

Use a specific component of the CMP to demonstrate how the CMP works and students' role in developing it.

Explain that students can develop a component of the CMP such as the homework policy. Ask them what a homework policy should tell a student and why such a policy is important, why it must be equitable, and why it must be enforced consistently. Explain that when a policy is in place, students know what is expected of them and know the consequences when they do not complete the homework. Introduce the homework policy in the CMP, and ask students to further develop it. Discuss the policy with students, and have them copy the policy in their notebooks. For younger students, place the policy on the bulletin board or a poster. Also, give students a copy to be signed by both the student and a parent and kept in their notebooks.

Closure

Ask students why the CMP is important and why the problem-solving strategies or homework policy or CMP will help them.

Teaching Classroom Rules

One of the first components of the CMP teachers should cover is classroom rules. Research supports establishing classroom rules early in the school year and allowing students to help create them. Students follow the rules they have developed more readily than those rules the teacher imposes on them. In addition, rules the class has developed collectively can engender class cohesiveness, strengthen student camaraderie, and support positive peer relationships (see also Figure 6.3).

Because the class develops the rules, this area of the CMP will require modification. When teaching rules or responsibilities, teachers may want to start with a CMP mini-lesson on why rules are important and what rules would benefit the class. During this lesson, students discuss and select the rules for their classroom. Teachers can plan a lesson for each rule or combine two or more rules into one lesson. Remember, in the teaching and learning of the CMP, the teacher and students must share their expectations. For example, the rule "Be respectful" can produce conflicting expectations among different populations. To a teacher, being respectful may mean staying in one's seat, doing what is asked the first time, or remaining quiet at all times. To students, being respectful may mean saying "please" and "thank you" or being helpful. Respect, to a student, may have no reference to staying in one's seat or not talking. Sharing these perspectives makes everyone more mindful of how to make a classroom work.

Sample CMP Mini-Lessons 2 and 3 are designed to help create and teach classroom rules.

Figure 6.3

The Rule of Five

Use the "rule of five" as a technique to remember the steps for making classroom rules. The five fingers serve as a reminder that five classroom rules are enough.

1. Looking at the thumb reminds the teacher that the class develops the rules.

2. Keeping the thumb raised, add the index finger, and recall that class rules must be brief, clear, and stated positively.

3. Adding the next finger reminds the teacher that class rules are to be posted, and students must memorize them.

4. Adding the fourth finger tells the teacher that class rules must be taught.

5. Raising the final finger reminds the teacher that class rules require a commitment from the students in the class. This commitment is that all students will follow the rules. This can be done by reaching a consensus, asking to have everyone raise their hand if they agree, or by signing a contract. All the students need to see that everyone agrees.

CMP MINI-LESSON FOR DEVELOPING CLASSROOM RULES

Grade: K–3

Time: 15 minutes

Materials

Coaching accoutrements such as a sweat suit and whistle

Objectives

Students will be able to

- identify words associated with coach.
- develop rules for working as a class team.
- work together in cooperative learning groups while establishing rules.

Opener

Enter the room wearing a sweat suit and baseball hat, with a whistle draped around your neck, and ask students, "Who am I?"

Instruction

After letting students guess your role, make a word web on the board, placing the word coach in the middle of the web, and ask students to provide words related to coach. Have students write these words in their journals.

Guide students to select such words as team, goals, coaching, players, uniforms, and hats. Ask if they see any similarities between a teacher and the coach of a team. List some similarities on the board. Next ask what similarities exist between them as students and members of a sports team. Again, list these similarities.

Once you feel students can see how the class is similar to a team, ask them to name some rules a team member on a basketball team must follow. A soccer team? List their answers on the board. Then give students the opportunity to identify one rule they think the class team would need to follow to win this year's trophy for Best Class. Place students in groups. If students sit at tables, tape a baseball sticker or small piece of paper with a computer-generated sports graphic on it to one chair. Or simply hand one student in each group a sticker or the graphic. The student with the sticker or graphic records the group's suggestion. Tell them they have five minutes to work. Monitor student understanding by asking students to repeat what you have asked them to do. Identify the a recorder for each group, and ask that student to explain his or her role. Ask students how long they have to complete the assignment and how many rules they are to submit.

Tell them you will time the activity, and when they have one minute left, you will write that on the board. When the time is up, you will ring a bell. Again, ask them how they will know when they have a minute left. And how will they know time is up? Finally, ask if they have any questions before they begin.

After sounding the time's-up bell, call on the recorders to report to the class their group's rule. Write these rules on the board or overhead projector. As a class, talk about the rules and select, by means of a democratic vote, the first rule in making the class team successful.

Closure

Ask why the first rule is an important one. Have students copy the rule into their journals, and write the rule on the rule board.

SAMPLE MINI-LESSON 3

CMP MINI-LESSON FOR TEACHING CLASSROOM RULES: RESPECT

Grade: 4–8

Time: 15 minutes

Materials

Recording of Aretha Franklin's "Respect"

Objectives

Students will be able to

- define respect.
- explain three ways to show respect in the classroom.

Opener

Play a recording of Aretha Franklin's "Respect." Point to each letter of the word on the rules poster as Aretha sings it. Ask if the song gives them any hints about the topic of today's lesson.

Instruction

Tell students they will create a working definition of respect for the class. Ask them what they think respect means, and place their answers in a web on the board. When they feel they have covered all of the major points, have them pair up with the person seated beside them for a think-pair-share activity. Tell them to decide on the most essential terms to describe or define respect and to be prepared to share their answer with the class in three minutes.

Ask for volunteers to share their group's ideas about the essential ingredients of respect. Write the terms on the board. Give students one minute to choose the term that is most important and the one that is second in importance to include in the definition. Number each term as students choose it: first choice, second choice, and so on.

Let students formulate the class definition. Then have students copy the definition into their journals or notebooks.

Now that the class has a definition of respect, ask them to consider another aspect of the word—who and what deserves respect. Have them list ways to show respect in the classroom and write their answers in their journal. Circulate among students and give positive feedback.

Have all students stand up. Tell them to remain standing if they have at least two ways to show respect on their list. Then have only those students with at least three ways on their list stay standing, then students with five ways on their list, then six, then eight, and finally, narrow the field to the one or two students with the most statements on their list. Have those students list their ways to show respect on the board.

Point out that many people, objects, and situations deserve respect. Ask if any student has a way to show respect that is not listed on the board, and, if so, add it to the list. Have students copy the list into their journal. Go down the list and discuss how one should show respect to these people or in these circumstances or situations.

Closure

Ask for a volunteer to state the class definition of respect. At the same time, point to the first objective of the lesson that is written on the board: students will be able to define respect. Ask the students to name a way everyone can show respect in the classroom. Point to the second objective on the board. Tell the class that they now know at least three ways to show respect in the classroom, and ask them why this is important.

Independent Practice

Have students write a paragraph explaining why respect is important in school and out of school.

Teaching Consequences

Place consequences in hierarchical order of severity. Begin with a non-verbal warning such as eye contact, proximity, or both. This first level is necessary because it serves as a reminder, doesn't stop instruction, and makes students accountable for their actions.

The second level in the consequence hierarchy is expressing a clear verbal warning such as stating the inappropriate behavior and supplying an appropriate one, using an I-statement, or having the class choose a word or cue that signals a student or students to discontinue the inappropriate behavior(s). An *I-statement* expresses one's thoughts and feelings about another's actions or words. An I-statement conveys three points to students: (1) the inappropriate behavior; (2) how the teacher feels about the behavior; and 3) why the behavior is causing a problem (Charles, 1999). In making an I-statement, follow this outline: I feel [tell the feeling] when you [say the reason] because [state the effect]; for example, "I feel frustrated when everyone talks at once because I can't hear what anyone is saying. Please raise your hand."

The class could choose a word, phrase, or cue that means, "Stop the inappropriate behavior now before it escalates beyond control." Examples of some words include "Freeze," meaning stop the behavior now; "Trouble in Paradise," meaning a problem exists; and "TLC," meaning everyone needs to offer **T**otal **L**earning **C**onsideration. Some cues include referee's signals and sign language. At this second level in the hierarchy, the student has one more opportunity to choose more appropriate behavior without disciplinary action.

The third level of the consequence hierarchy is a cooling off period, sometimes called a time-out. This period provides students an opportunity to collect themselves by going to a planned place in the room or another room for a specified amount of time. Instead of a time-out, the teacher may, at this third level, decide to plan a conference with the student to discuss how the student could avoid reaching this level in the future. The teacher could choose to make a telephone call to the parent or arrange a conference with the student and his or her parents.

The fourth level may be a demerit, conduct notice, in-school suspension, or similar consequence. The fifth and final level may be a visit with the principal. Teachers can create their own hierarchy of consequences themselves or solicit student input. If a student presents such major discipline problems as fighting, hitting, or throwing objects, the student does not progress through the hierarchy but the teacher enforces the most severe consequence or most appropriate level of the hierarchy.

Teach the consequences and the hierarchy to students. Get a commitment that they understand and agree with the consequences just as they gave their commitment to the rules. Whenever students have input into the components of the CMP, the teacher must include in the CMP mini-lesson the call for consensus and a show of commitment.

Discuss both the CMP and the consequence hierarchy with the principal at the beginning of the year. A principal can be an effective part of the CMP when this person knows when he or she will be called into the plan. The lesson plan below can assist teachers in teaching consequences.

CMP MINI-LESSON FOR TEACHING CONSEQUENCES

Grade: 2–6

Time: 20 minutes

Materials

Class rules poster, consequence list

Objectives

Students will be able to

- recognize that consequences exist when they break the rules.
- explain the escalating consequences for continually breaking the rules.

Opener

With the poster of Class Rules in a prominent position, ask the class which of the class rules they think is most important. Write their answers on the board. Then take a vote. Say, for example, the class agrees that "Respect" is the most important rule to make the classroom a place where all can learn and work together. Have students list all the reasons respect is vital in the classroom. Tell them the class will discuss what happens when that rule, or any one of the other class rules, is broken.

Instruction

Discuss how someone who is not following the respect rule might be behaving. Perhaps this person is talking and interrupting the teacher or making it difficult for fellow students to hear or to work. Ask students what the class should do in that situation. Should the class let the behavior continue? Should something be done to the rule-breaker? Should the student be chastised by the teacher? Sent to the principal? Be suspended?

Have students work in pairs to decide what should be done to the rule-breaker. Have students share their answers with the class, and list them on the board.

Discuss whether a student who has broken the rule only once should have to suffer the same consequences as someone who has broken the rule many times or broken many rules.

Post the hierarchy of consequences for rule infractions and discuss the levels. Read the list and demonstrate some of the consequences; for example, the first time you notice a student disrupting the class, you give a nonverbal warning. An example of a nonverbal warning is eye contact with the student. If the student doesn't cooperate after the first warning, he or she gets another chance to follow the rule.

Next, move very near a student and ask the class to describe the action. Ask if they think standing right on top of the student's desk will help quiet the rule-breaker. What should happen if the rule-breaker stops the behavior after either "The Look" or the "Close-Up"? Listen to class suggestions, and then say that anyone who takes the hint and stops talking or disrupting the class after a nonverbal warning will be fine. If the behavior doesn't stop, the next level is necessary. Ask students to explain *why* the next level is necessary.

Explain that the second level is a verbal warning. If the chatty classmate does not take the nonverbal hints, you might say something like, "I feel disappointed when you talk when I'm giving instructions, Joe, because you are making it hard for the people around you to concentrate on what we're trying to learn." If Joe stops talking and settles down for the rest of the day, nothing more will happen. Ask the class if the rule-breaker should suffer a consequence if he continues to cause problems. Point to the third level on the hierarchy of consequences.

For younger grades, try using a Behavior Stoplight: All students have a car with their name on it. There is a large class Behavior Stoplight on a bulletin board and kids have their cars randomly placed all over one side of the bulletin board. When a student breaks a rule, such as talking when the teacher is giving instructions, he or she gets the car and moves it from green to amber on the Behavior Stoplight. This means the student has a warning. The next time the student talks while the teacher is giving instructions or breaks another classroom rule, the student has to move his or her car from amber to red. If the student is told to move to the red light, he or she will know this behavior is unacceptable and must choose a more appropriate behavior. The student moves the car and places a check by his or her name on the Traffic Control poster. One check means the student moves to the time-out chair for five minutes, the student signs the traffic ticket book, and a teacher–student conference is scheduled; two checks means a note home, and three an immediate telephone call home. Good behavior earns the child a green light and he or she may return to traveling with the other cars.

For older students, the rule-breaker must go to a time-out place and complete "The Note," which is a blank form with various sections. Joe must explain how he broke the classroom rule and what he could do differently next time, and sign a pledge to try to behave more appropriately. The completed form documents the student's behavior. If the student must complete a second note, both notes are sent home with a letter from the teacher explaining the situation, asking for the parents' support in correcting the child's behavior, and requesting the parents' signature. The teacher shows the students a blank copy of The Note and explains the sections that need to be completed.

Ask if everyone feels this is fair treatment. Get class consensus. If a student feels some unfairness, the student must explain why and suggest another way. The class discusses the new option and chooses between what the student has suggested or what had been suggested earlier.

Explain that the final level is a visit to the principal. Express the wish that they avoid that step.

Closure

Ask students to describe what happens the first time someone does not honor the respect rule, and if he or she doesn't take the nonverbal hint. What might the rule-breaker hear if the activity continues? If the behavior still doesn't stop, what happens? How can writing The Note help a student? What is the last final step?

Teaching Incentives

Spend time thinking about incentives. Incentives are inducements from teachers to students, ranging from simple ones such as high fives, winks, thumbs up, and talk time to more elaborate gestures, opportunities, and experiences such as homework passes, Freedom Friday, field trips, guest speakers, and sign language instruction.

The classroom incentives portion of the CMP needs student input, so this area will change somewhat based on that input. It is important to note that incentives, like rules and consequences, need a classroom show of agreement and commitment—a show of hands, contract, or other pact. All members of the class then work toward earning the agreed-upon incentives. Given this role in how the class operates, it becomes the students' class, not the teacher's class. This sense of student control, power, and autonomy supports how a classroom works and how teachers and students work in a classroom (see Figure 6.4).

Remember, the goal is for students to choose the incentives readily over the consequences, to buy into the CMP instead of ignoring or rebelling against it. Thus, the incentives need to reflect student ownership, autonomy, and empowerment. The following CMP mini-lesson plan is one example of teaching classroom incentives to students.

Figure 6.4

The Teacher Who Always Wore Pants

In one classroom, the class-selected incentive pertained to collecting compliments. Students decided that if the class received 10 compliments, the teacher would perform one cartwheel. Students decided the more compliments, the more cartwheels. The compliments came from school staff, teachers, and parents. Students all worked together to be good in order to see the teacher do cartwheels. The teacher earned the reputation as the Cartwheel Teacher, and kids couldn't wait to get into her class so as to be good and earn compliments.

SAMPLE MINI-LESSON 5

CMP MINI-LESSON FOR TEACHING INCENTIVES

Grade: 1–8

Time: 15–20 minutes

Materials

Jar, marbles

Objectives

Students will be able to

- identify appropriate behaviors that can earn marbles.
- recognize the cue for getting their attention.
- apply the marble jar incentive to classroom management and learning.

Opener

Hold up a jar. Hold up a package of marbles. Explain that Jar + Marbles = Incentive. Ask students what incentives are and why they are important. Ask them to guess how this jar will work in this classroom. Explain that the marble jar will collect earned "recognitions" and when it's filled, the class receives recognition for a job well done (adapted from Canter & Canter, 1976).

Instruction

Discuss how individual students and the class can earn marbles. When students or the class behave well, a marble or two goes into the jar. Ask students what behaviors might be worth a marble or two. Have the class make a list and copy the list into their notebooks, or place students into groups of two or more, and have each group identify five appropriate behaviors. Record the behaviors on the board.

Share specific examples of how students and the class can earn marbles. Discuss how they can help each other earn marbles. The following specific examples apply to grades 4 to 8.

- Exhibiting good behavior in the halls and going to and from special events
- Displaying good citizenship
- Working diligently and productively on assignments
- Demonstrating good behavior in assemblies and other events outside of class
- Receiving compliments from others
- Honoring the class rules
- Following directions, routines, and procedures correctly
- Solving problems and making good choices

Place a few marbles in the jar and shake it, making a sound everyone can hear. Explain that when students hear this sound, they should stop all work and give full attention to the teacher. The marble jar also serves as a cue for getting students' attention.

Have students decide (vote) on the reward they will receive when the jar is filled. This marble jar incentive supports the entire CMP.

Closure

Ask students to explain how the marble jar works in this classroom. If they speak out of turn or do not raise their hands, shake the marble jar and see if they respond to the cue. If they do, drop their first earned marble into the jar.

Teaching Social Skills

Many communities expect schools to focus more attention on developing social and cooperative student behaviors. Sylwester (1995) reminds educators how important it is to help students learn skills of cooperation. He states, "In our multicultural society, the school is the place where children from diverse backgrounds come together, and thus it is the best place for them to learn to work well with others" (p. 118). If students pick on one another, say cruel things, complain, whine, and tattle, teachers should plan mini-lessons to develop more appropriate social behavior, strengthening interpersonal skills, and stressing the three Cs: cooperation, consideration, and civility. Sample CMP Mini-Lessons 6 and 7 have been developed to teach social skills.

CMP MINI-LESSON FOR TEACHING SOCIAL SKILLS: FRIENDSHIP AND RESPECT

Grade: K–3

Time: 30 minutes

Materials

The Giving Tree, by Shel Silverstein

Per student: 5" × 8" sheet of white unlined paper; 9" × 12" sheet of colored construction paper; 10 four-inch squares of brown tissue paper; 10 four-inch squares of light blue tissue paper; 20 squares of green tissue paper, paintbrush; half-glue and half-water mixture; glue; scissors; and pencil, crayons, or markers

Objectives

Students will be able to

- define friendship and how it works.
- describe ways to make and keep friends.

Opener

Before this lesson, send a note home explaining the lesson and asking that each child bring in a small item they can give to a friend such as a drawing, painting,, or something they baked.

Read aloud *The Giving Tree* by Shel Silverstein to give students an understanding of the word *giving.* Ask students to each tell how they feel when someone gives them a present.

Instruction

Start with a semantic web of student definitions of friendship, and discuss the book *The Giving Tree.*

Discuss different actions and situations in which people make friends and keep them. Have students get into their think-pair-share groups and come up with three acts of friendship.

Introduce friendship cards and explain using squares of colored tissue paper to form pictures. Explain that this is called a mosaic. Show examples of mosaics in an art book or a teacher-made example. Have students work in groups of four to make their own cards.

To make Friendship Cards, brush a mixture of half glue and half water on the center of the white paper. Place brown tissue paper on the wet area, overlapping the squares to make a tree trunk. Continue adding the glue-water mixture and tissue squares to make a tree scene with leaves (green), grass (green), and sky (blue). Brush the entire picture with the glue-water mixture. Let the picture dry. Trim the tissue squares from the edges of the white paper as needed. Fold construction paper in half to make a card. Glue the tissue paper picture to the front of the card.

Let students write a special message in the card for a friend.

Closure

Review each item the tree gives to the boy in the story. Have each child think of something he or she could do to make a friend happy. Have every student draw another student's name out of a box, and give the special item they brought to that person. Ask students what they learned.

Independent Practice

Have students write in their journals about their very best friend. Have them describe what a friend is, why they like their friend, and what they do for their friend.

SAMPLE MINI-LESSON 7

CMP MINI-LESSON FOR TEACHING SOCIAL SKILLS: CLASS MEETINGS

Grade: 6–12

Time: 10–15 minutes

Materials

Audiotape of stock market traders, T-chart with "Class Meeting Behaviors" printed at the top

Objectives

Students will be able to

- describe a class meeting.
- identify good class meeting behaviors.
- create four class meeting rules.

Opener

Play a 30-second excerpt of a tape of the stock market during trading time, with all of its seeming confusion. Ask students to take a minute to write down words that describe the scene.

Instruction

Begin a discussion from the words they have written and ask about behaviors that may help you work together as a class. Next, describe what a class meeting is and how it works. Make a chart labeled "Class Meeting Behaviors," to record student answers.

Ask students to take a minute to think about the kinds of behaviors that are necessary for good class meetings. Have students pair up with their neighbor and for two minutes compile a list of proper behaviors for class meetings. Ask the pairs to share the behaviors with the class. Write them on the chart and have students copy them into their notebook. Have students form groups of four—two sets of pairs—and begin devising four class meeting rules. Have the groups share their ideas with the whole class, discuss them, choose four, and vote on the rules. Place the rules for class meetings on a poster to be displayed permanently in the classroom.

Closure

Ask students how these behaviors help conduct business at a class meeting. Discuss what a teacher can do to support these rules and what students can do to support them.

Teaching Cues

Cues engender a response from students faster than words. Students often view teachers as talking too much, with students required to listen to every word. Nonverbal cues are quick, fun, and effective, and students like to figure them out by themselves without being told what to do.

It is essential to develop one cue to get everyone's attention. Another important cue is one that places students into prearranged groups quickly and without discussion. An example of a cue for group work is to raise the index finger, which means students will work in their assigned think-pair-share partner arrangement. Raising the index finger and the next finger together means work with your table or row, whichever is appropriate. Raising four fingers means students should work in the group they are assigned to this month, and the extended hand means students should work in their own preselected groups of four students.

Sample Mini-Lessons 8 and 9 focus on teaching cues to the class.

CMP MINI-LESSON FOR TEACHING CUES

Grade: K–3

Time: 20 minutes

Objective

Students will be able to

- recognize the classroom cue.
- apply the five actions needed to follow it.

Opener

Draw a giant-sized hand on the chalkboard.

Instruction

Explain to students that your outstretched hand and your five fingers, along with the words "Give me Five," will be the class cue, and you will use it to get the entire class's attention immediately; then show them the five fingers of simple directions. Have students hold their hands up in the air while you explain the five steps they must take when you say, "Give me five!"

As you state each action, hold up one finger for each direction. The five actions are (1) Eyes on me, (2) Mouths quiet, (3) Bodies still, (4) Hands closed, and (5) Listen to me (adapted from Wong & Wong, 1998).

Give students sample scenarios; for example, say "If I'm listening, sitting still, being quiet with my hands to myself, am I following the cue? Did I leave something out?" They should respond, "You forgot eyes on you!" While you teach this cue, randomly say "Give me five!" Check how many students are watching you and listening and following the finger directions. Each time you say the cue; review the five actions with students: Am I looking at the teacher? Is my mouth quiet? Is my body still? Are my hands closed? Am I listening?

Students enjoy repeating these phrases many times, and they will learn the five steps through repetition.

Closure

Have students repeat the five actions and ask a few students to write them on the board in each of the fingers. Have students continue to practice this cue. Eventually, students will keep themselves and their peers accountable for this cue each time they hear or see it.

Independent Practice

Have students trace their hands and label the fingers with the directions.

CMP MINI-LESSON FOR TEACHING CUES

Grade: 4 and 5

Time: 15 minutes

Materials

Graduation gown, gavel

Objectives

Students will be able to

- identify the purpose of a classroom cue.
- devise a classroom cue.

Opener

Dress in a black graduation gown and hold a gavel. Ask, "Who am I?" and "What's this?" Provide a short clip from the television program "Judge Judy."

Instruction

Ask students to describe what a judge does. Why does a judge need a gavel? Write student responses on the board. Ask students if order in the courtroom is important. Why or why not? Ask them if order is also important in the classroom, and why or why not.

Ask the class, if a judge uses a gavel to get attention and order in the courtroom, what should a teacher use in the classroom to get attention and order? Have students come up with the best "gavel" for the classroom, such as a whistle, bell, or clap sequence, then call their choice a cue. List their cue ideas on the board, and vote for the best one. Ask when you should use the cue. Write their responses on the board. Tell students that for order and safety, it is imperative that the cue works. Ask them to raise their right hand and repeat the following: "I promise to uphold the cue of our classroom with the utmost respect and honor by following its purpose."

Closure

Ask students why it is important for a class to have a cue. Have them describe the class cue.

Teaching With a Computer

In addition to arranging desks, establishing reading corners, and preparing learning centers, today's teachers must plan computer areas. As the ratio of students to computers may be at best 25:2 in a classroom, it takes a commitment to technology and advance planning by the teacher to use computers in teaching and the learning of lessons. Student use of computers, like learning centers, must reflect scheduled assigned groups. Teachers might, for example, schedule groups of students to work on computers by the days of the week as shown in the chart in Figure 6.5.

Figure 6.5

	Mon.	Tues.	Wed.	Thurs.	Fri.
Group 1	Computer	Read text	Worksheet	Teacher	Project
Group 2	Teacher	Read text	Computer	Worksheet	Project
Group 3	Read text	Teacher	Worksheet	Computer	Project
Group 4	Read text	Computer	Teacher	Worksheet	Project
Group 5	Read text	Worksheet	Project	Teacher	Computer

SAMPLE MINI-LESSON 10

CMP MINI-LESSON FOR TEACHING WITH A COMPUTER

Grade: 1–5

Time: 20 minutes

Materials

Bow-tie pasta (one piece for each student), clear plastic container

Objectives

Students will be able to

- review the computer programs available on the classroom computer.
- develop autonomy while taking turns on the computer.

Opener

Give each student one piece of bow-tie pasta. Have students write their student number on the noodle. (The number can be teacher-assigned or their number in the grade book.) Have them decorate their noodle around the number, then put all the pasta into a clear plastic container.

Instruction

Ask students why people use computers and why they are so important. Make a semantic web of their responses, and have students copy the web. Explain to students that the classroom has a computer center for them to use every morning. Provide an overview of the classroom's software programs.

To determine who will use the computer at certain times, place the container holding the pasta on the computer table. Explain that during computer center time, you will choose two pieces of pasta, and the two students with the numbers chosen will use the computers for 20 minutes. Explain that you will continue choosing two pieces of pasta throughout the morning of each day to ensure that all students have time at the computer during the week. Plan for six students a day to use the computer center. Use a timer to keep track of the time.

Closure

Ask students to explain the procedure for computer use and copy it into their journals.

Independent Practice

Have students continue to follow this system of taking turns on the computer throughout the year. After a day or two, make students responsible for picking the pasta. This schedule enables them to work independently because they know what to do.

Revising the Classroom Management Plan

Every evening when she got home from school, Joan took her two dogs, Max and Spencer, for a walk. They walked along the creek near Johnson's farm, and while the boys romped and chased squirrels, Joan took advantage of the fresh air, the pastoral setting, and the time alone to reflect on her classes that day. She replayed the day in her mind's eye, thinking about what had gone wrong and what had gone right. On this particular evening, she thought about a student who was struggling. When the dogs were tired from their play, they sat next to her on the grass under their favorite old tree, and she stroked them and wondered how she could help Stephen, who spent most of the time when he should have been writing in his journal doodling in its margins. He had a talent for drawing, that was clear, but how could she help him put that talent to use in her English class? By the time the dogs had gotten restless and were ready to head for home and their dinner bowls, she had devised a plan for him to draw a cartoon strip for the next writing assignment. When she reached home, she felt refreshed and invigorated. She took a few minutes to jot down ideas for the next day's lessons and wrote herself a note to talk with Stephen tomorrow. Her head clear, she walked into to the kitchen for dinner.

A PLAN IN FLUX

The CMP is a dynamic plan that thrives on reflection and revision. Changing and improving the CMP provides an opportunity for professional growth and development. It is not a plan teachers can carve in stone and display in the classroom for all to read. Rather, it is more like clay teachers mold to suit their experience and their students. In thinking about working with some children that are very alienated from the school and everything it represents, or whose experience of school has been one of massive failure, a CMP may not be able to fix all the problems but it serves as a way to begin to address those serious issues. When students bring into the classrooms such problems as drugs and alcohol and conditions seen as emotional and psychological disorders, a teacher must seek outside help or utilize a stricter, more teacher-centered approach in both planning and revising the CMP.

The final phase of the classroom management process is revision of the CMP. A teacher takes scheduled time for reflection, examines the current classroom problems, and looks for the connection between what is going on in the classroom and the contents of the CMP. Reflection provides the impetus to change—it can be the vision teachers need to modify, revise, and try again. Teachers must reflect and revise on a routine basis. A Chesapeake, Virginia, teacher of the year, Lindsay Crump Porzio, writes,

> Each year, I reflect on the following story and I renew my commitment to each and every student in my class:
>
> A retiring builder was asked to build one last house. Anxious to finish quickly, the builder used cheap materials and poor workmanship. When he finished, his employer handed him the keys and said, "Congratulations! This is your new house." The builder was shocked that he was to live in the poorly built house. If only he had built it better.
>
> As teachers, we are the builders of the future and our "houses" are the young minds and spirits of children. Always we must use the best materials and organize our lessons with quality teaching moments. Every day we must ask ourselves, "Could I have done this better?" When we are handed the "keys," our reaction should be satisfaction. The future we build will be ours and that of the students.

Teachers must continue to expand and develop their CMP. Not every decision or action teachers choose will work. Teachers learn with each success as well as with each failure, and they continue to improve their techniques. At the same time, they improve their methods for refining and implementing their plan. A teacher never needs to start a CMP from scratch again—just modify, improve, and continually strengthen it. This improvement occurs not only on paper but also is in the teacher.

REFLECTIVE REVISING OF THE CMP

Within the CMP lies the key to improving how the class works. The reflective revising procedure starts with the teacher reflecting on the CMP to ascertain the amount of student input that is found throughout the plan.

Next, the teacher reviews the four components of the CMP—classroom organization, instruction, evaluation, and professional development—to determine the connection of each component to Glasser's identified student needs. Finally, the teacher searches for the overlapping support of ideas from one component to another.

Reflect on the CMP for Student Input

First, identify which of the components of the CMP need student involvement and input and, therefore, need to be developed in the classroom. Classroom management that has student involvement creates more student on-task behavior and accountability to classroom teaching and learning. Teachers must engage in meaningful dialogue with students in revising the CMP. Each class, each year, is different, which means the CMP requires new teacher and student input to be effective and relevant. Allowing students to have a role in the development of the CMP takes time, but the rewards are many. For a more relevant and meaningful CMP, reflect on the components that need student involvement and input such as rules, procedures, cues, and incentives. Take the CMP to the classroom at the start of the school year, and ask the students for the needed input.

Review the CMP to Connect Components to Students' Needs

Second, review each component of the CMP and connect this information to Glasser's identified student needs. Glasser (as quoted in Charles, 1999) maintains,

> All human beings have genetic needs for (1) survival (food, shelter, freedom from harm); (2) belonging (security, comfort, legitimate membership in the group); (3) power (sense of importance, of stature, of being considered by others); (4) fun (having a good time, emotionally and intellectually); and (5) freedom (exercise of choice, self-direction, and responsibility). (p. 186)

Glasser (quoted in Charles, 2005) stresses that teachers must plan to meet these needs in a classroom. He says that

> students' need related to survival is met when the school environment is kept safe and free from personal threat. They sense belonging when they are involved in class matters, receive attention from the teacher and others, and are brought into discussions of matters that concern the class. Students sense power when the teacher asks them to participate in decisions about topics to be studied and procedures for working in the class. A sense of power also comes from being assigned responsibility for class duties, such as helping take attendance, caring for class animals, helping distribute and take care of materials, being in charge of audiovisual equipment, and so

forth. Students experience fun when they are able to work and talk with others, engage in interesting activities, and share their accomplishments. And they sense freedom when the teacher allows them to make responsible choices concerning what they will study, how they will do so, and how they will demonstrate their accomplishments. (p. 78)

Edwards (1997) contends that a comprehensive classroom plan that provides for students' basic needs is an important way to prevent discipline problems. Viewing the classroom management plan's four components and their ideas through the screen of students' needs will present areas that necessitate change.

Reflect on the CMP to Increase the Support of Ideas From One Component to Another

Third, examine the CMP for the support found among the components and their ideas. This integration of ideas results in the support of each idea by other ideas in other places in the CMP. When the CMP includes student input, when it meets student needs, and when it weaves support of one idea with others in the plan, students can't help but follow the plan. It just happens! Tracing the integration of one CMP component and its listed ideas with another component and its ideas usually results in adding ideas or strengthening the connection between or among ideas to ensure support of one another. For example, if one of the classroom rules is "Be prepared for class," look for support of this rule throughout the CMP (see Figure 7.1).

If students are not following a certain classroom rule or all of the rules, trace each rule through the CMP and strengthen the connections to the other components. An idea or rule standing in isolation with no support within the CMP usually fails. The integration of components and ideas

Figure 7.1

Rule 1: Be Prepared for Class

To look for support for the rule "Be prepared for class" throughout the CMP, begin by reviewing the Classroom Organization component. Is this rule supported by a routine or procedure? If a routine or procedure listed in the CMP supports this rule, go to another component and look for support for the rule. However, if no procedure supports this rule, add one to your CMP; for example, "When the bell rings, students must have their journals opened, have two sharpened pencils on their desks, and begin their daily journal entry. Students have 10 minutes to write. When the bell rings the second time, the row captain picks up the journals and places them in the row bin."

Continue with this reflection by looking at the room arrangement, bulletin board ideas, and the class motto. Do they support the "Be prepared for class" rule? Are incentives linked to the rule? Making these connections strengthens the effectiveness and efficiency of the CMP.

creates a situation whereby students follow the rules naturally; it is just how the classroom works. Next, look at the incentives and see if the plan supports them throughout. Take each component of the CMP and trace the integration of ideas. Finally, evaluate the overall components and the ideas expressed in the CMP. Some ideas may need to be added, modified, or omitted from the plan.

Seventh-grade teacher Lauren Peters sets aside time in her weekly schedule at school to reflect. She stops everything and first thinks about what is going well. Then she concentrates on a teaching or learning area that needs improvement. She recalls a problem pertaining to a cooperative learning activity. Lauren reflects on the situation and determines that her goal is to reduce the noise, decrease student movement in the room, and raise group productivity. Reviewing her CMP, she asks herself, "Do I have a rule that addresses noise, being considerate of others, staying in your groups, or producing quality work?" If she doesn't, now would be the time to plan a CMP mini-lesson in which the class adds a new rule or two to support cooperative working situations. But Lauren does have such a rule: "Keep noise down to a considerate level." She decides that a CMP mini-lesson for developing students' social skills is needed. In that lesson, the students will discuss the word *considerate* and reach a consensus on a definition and expectations for that word.

Reflecting on her CMP and Glasser's identified student needs, she asks herself the following questions: Does the classroom meet each of these needs? Do my students need more direction, more specific procedures, or more appropriate assignments for group work? What components and ideas in my CMP could I strengthen or add that would support more successful cooperative learning activity?

Next, Lauren thinks about what she can do to reduce the noise and foster more acceptable and productive work behavior. She ponders several options, including establishing a cue, developing rules for working relationships, or assigning roles in group work—in particular, a role for one student to monitor the noise level of the group.

She reviews the CMP components and decides she will add an incentive for students to demonstrate more effort and produce quality work. She double-checks the group incentives component to ensure that such recognition exists.

Lauren's final step in the reflective revising of her CMP is to strengthen and maintain its efficient and effective operation in her classroom. She recognizes that a CMP must reflect the changing needs of the class and remain a dynamic plan for classroom management.

SUMMARY OF THE REFLECTIVE REVISING PROCESS

Teachers need to be mindful that the CMP is a work in progress. The following ideas are helpful in providing a quick review of the revising process:

- Add student ideas or strategies to the CMP. Provide more ways to collect student input as well as class information from such activities as get-acquainted games, interest surveys, show and tell, and so forth. With student input in hand, look for more ways to continually personalize the CMP.
- Review Glasser's student needs for survival, belonging, power, fun, and freedom, and attempt to provide more connections by including more opportunities, possibilities, and experiences in the CMP components to meet those student needs.
- Examine the four components and their ideas in the CMP and locate the areas that require strengthening or need more support to resolve the current situation. Once again, develop more support by integrating ideas in each component with ideas in other components.
- Visit a colleague or two in your school and complete another Observation Guide. Think about the collected information in terms of your CMP. Integrate some fresh ideas into your CMP.

When teachers add or strengthen components, ideas, and strategies in the CMP, the new material must then be taught. Once again, teach the materials using CMP mini-lessons and gain the commitment to the new input with student consensus. The CMP remains a work in progress.

8

Samples of Effective Teachers' Classroom Management Plans

When Bruce Gibson, an education major and preservice teacher, turned his CMP in to Professor Warburton, the professor found the following note attached to the plan.

"Dear Professor," it began. "I spent a lot of time on my CMP, and the more I thought about its content, the more I realized I had still more to think about, and the more I wrote, the more I realized how little I know about classroom management.

"So I turn this in because today is the due date, not because I am entirely satisfied with the product. Even as I placed it in your mailbox, I could see areas I wanted to revise. I guess what I'm saying is, as you review my plan, please understand that it is still a work in progress. I'm sure that by the time I step foot into my own classroom for the first time, I will have revised it, and by the time my first year of teaching is complete, it may, in fact, bear only a resemblance to the plan you now hold."

Professor Warburton smiled. He couldn't have asked for anything more. Bruce was going to be all right.

ON SOLID GROUND WITH A CMP

No two CMPs are alike—each is unique to the teacher who composes it. According to Wong (1990), the central difference between novice and experienced teachers is that successful teachers feel comfortable and in control of the teaching environment. The classroom management process provides the beginning teacher with the foundation on which those feelings of competence and self-assurance form. For the practicing teacher, the classroom management process provides a guide to organize one's thoughts, behaviors, and practices into the CMP.

Ideas for a CMP are everywhere, and when they discover good ideas, good teachers add to and refine the CMP. The classroom management process makes it simple to structure classroom management into teaching and student learning and create a sense of community in the classroom. Teachers can replace the phrase "Some teachers have it and others do not" with "I can make classroom management happen!"

The following sample CMPs have been developed by both preservice teachers and practicing teachers. CMPs are included for all grade levels: primary (K–3), intermediate (4 and 5), middle (6–8), and secondary (9–12).

SAMPLE PLAN 1

SAMPLE CMP FOR PRIMARY GRADES

My Personal Classroom Management Plan

Grade Level: *Primary*

Teaching Goal: *My job is to ensure that every child who comes through my classroom door feels he or she is special and knows that I care.*

CLASSROOM ORGANIZATION

Classroom Environment

Draw or describe room arrangement

> *The room is arranged so all students can easily see the chalkboard and Word Wall. The carpet area is used for whole-group instruction, cooperative groups, and oral reading (Figure 8.1).*

Figure 8.1

Sketch bulletin board ideas

Figure 8.2

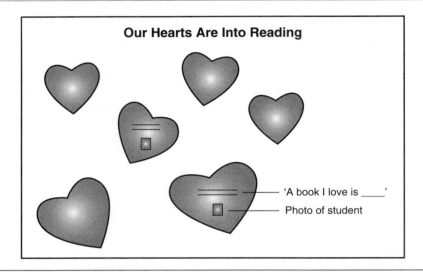

Class motto

> *The class motto is to treat others as you want to be treated.*

Classroom Operation

Rules

> *Always be a good listener.*
>
> *Raise your hand and wait to be called upon.*
>
> *Keep your hands and feet to yourself.*
>
> *Respect others and their belongings.*
>
> *Follow directions.*

Routines and procedures

> *Every morning, students organize themselves for the day, including bringing notes to me, unpacking books, and sharpening pencils. I write any important messages on the board for students to read in the morning.*
>
> *Students put any homework into the appropriate homework tray and any notes from home into the teacher's "in" box.*
>
> *We write in our journals for 15 minutes daily, teacher included.*
>
> *After school announcements, I take attendance and lunch count. A student helper delivers the attendance card and lunch count to the appropriate place.*
>
> *The class takes bathroom breaks according to the daily schedule, ideally, after lunch and before or after resource times. Students may get water at these times.*

For emergency bathroom breaks, students are instructed not to ask to leave during a lesson but may ask during independent work time.

Students sharpen two pencils in the morning. If their pencil breaks during the day, they set it in the "sharpen cup" on their desk, and one of the class helpers sharpens all these at an appropriate time.

Students are encouraged to complete work in a timely fashion. For students who finish early, various center activities are available to reinforce skills appropriate to the time. Students are also, on occasion, required to read silently or take accelerated reader (if applicable) tests. If the assignment allows for student helpers, students who finish early might be asked to assist those still working.

A Word Wall helps students with spelling. If a word is not found on the wall, students are encouraged to sound the word out or look it up in a dictionary.

In getting ready for lunch, students line up as follows: baggers buying nothing, baggers buying milk or dessert, those buying lunch according to their lunch choice, and according to rows/tables for popular lunch items.

I try to devote at least 15 minutes three times weekly to math games during math time because children learn through play, and math games reinforce important skills in an entertaining manner.

All resource classes are observed, and I schedule in a daily recess time to give students a needed breather.

For the last few minutes of the day, I allow "talk time" with the radio playing quietly if students earn this through positive behavior.

Students must follow rules when working in cooperative groups. I teach "Rules for Working Together" along with cues such as "Give me five" and others to get students' attention.

The class holds weekly class meetings; a clipboard is posted for students to write questions and problems.

Students have stop signs on sticks, which they place in a personally decorated can that is on their desk when they need teacher assistance during silent work time or tests. They work silently until I can get to them.

At the end of the day, students get time to pack up at their desk, and then they are called by sections to get their belongings from the coat rack.

Students are dismissed from their seats when called to go home. Students stack the chairs before leaving the room.

Consequences

Students are introduced to a behavior program at the beginning of the year in which they "change the cards" for inappropriate behaviors. Every day students start with a blue card. If they have to be spoken to for inappropriate behavior, the following occurs: first, a warning; second, change card to yellow; third, change card to red and write a "think paper" to go home to parents about their behavior (parents sign the card, and students return it); fourth, referral to the principal's office.

Any severe behavior problems are referred to the principal immediately.

Incentives

I drop marbles into a small jar when students exhibit good conduct.

During warm weather, students earn free time on Friday by earning letters that spell RECESS. Appropriate behavior as a class earns them a letter. If all letters are earned by Friday, free time is awarded.

For individual rewards, students try to be "caught being good." Behaviors that are rewarded include being on task, walking quietly in the halls, doing what is asked of them, and being kind to others. Students receive a slip of paper and put their name on it. At the end of the day, any slips received are deposited into a class treasure chest. At the end of the week, one name is drawn and that person chooses a special prize. Then all names are discarded, and an empty chest starts the next week.

Students also receive happy grams for good test scores, awesome behavior, or kind deeds done unto others. These are sent home with students for parents to see.

Students receive tokens or stamps to place on a "Thumbs Up" poster when "caught being good" to activate the positive ripple effect.

Other incentives are a popcorn party, ice cream social, free time, or lunch in the classroom.

Cues

To regain class attention I use the following cues:

The phrase "Stop, look, and listen." Students freeze.

The phrase "All eyes on me." Students stop what they are doing.

Hand raised silently in the air—refocus attention on me.

Positive ripple effect: "I like the way Joe has his book opened to the right page, notebook opened, and pencil sharpened." Others try to do the same thing to get recognition.

Lights Out: students understand this signals an emergency announcement.

Hand signals for group arrangements

A rap

INSTRUCTION

Lessons

Instructional strategies

Students have opportunities for individual, pair, and group learning experiences.

Use portfolios to monitor success.

Through cooperative learning activities, students learn to assume responsibilities and work efficiently with others.

Use hands-on learning.

Use computer to review basic skills.

Allow students to discuss work with peers.

Use constant visual checks for assessing students' understanding of the lesson while teaching—for example, ask a question and have students respond either with a "thumbs up" or down or sideways or by sitting or standing to get a visual check.

Teach lessons that allow for active student participation.

Have good openers to lessons and closure.

Write objectives on the corner of the chalkboard.

Use videotapes, audiotapes, and computer.

Individualized instructional strategies

Provide feedback immediately after class takes a test.

Students have the opportunity to read to me on several occasions.

Create different assignments for alternative learners.

Issue contracts for learning.

Provide help sessions.

Schedule volunteers to assist students.

Hold flex groups for small-group learning.

Provide enrichment activities.

Allow students to choose some work to add to their portfolio.

Use individual file folders for practice.

Assessment strategies

Thumbs Up

White Boards

Questions and Answers

Questioning strategies

Ask divergent and convergent questions.

Allow students time to compose their answers (see Figure 4.8).

Allow students to say "pass or play" when answering questions.

Use calling sticks to call on students randomly.

Ask preview and predict questions.

Ask why and what if questions—higher-level questions.

Ask, "Does anyone want to add to this answer?"

Examples of questions

What is figurative language?

Cite some examples from Amelia Bedelia.

Can you put this definition in your own words?

What was the most important issue facing the Puritans? Why?

Compare and contrast these ideas.

What might it be like in 2050?

What is your opinion on this issue?

What do you think about this topic? Why?

Find the evidence in your textbook.

Responses to students

When a student gives a correct answer:

"Excellent."

"Good job."

Give a smile and a thumbs up.

Use praise words such as "Exactly!" and "Yes!"

When a student gives a partially correct answer:

"What else can you tell me?"

"You are on the right track."

"Keep thinking and I will come back to you."

"Close. Can anyone else help?"

When a student gives an incorrect answer:

"Let me give you some more information."

"Wait a minute. Think about this, and I will come back to you."

"Keep listening, and let's see what you come up with."

Student self-evaluation opportunities

Check homework with a partner.

Use answer keys.

Choose work to place in their portfolio.

Use calculators.

Have informal conferences with teacher.

Effective Teaching Practices

Building positive relationships

Between teacher and students

Before the school year begins, students receive invitation postcards from me. On the first day of school, I share a little about myself by bringing in some personal items that describe and show them the type of person I am. Students are invited to bring in something to share about themselves on the days that follow.

Students complete an interest survey during the first weeks of school. I use these to learn the likes and dislikes of my students.

When possible, I greet students at the door in the morning and say good-bye to them as they leave in the afternoon.

Occasionally, students are invited to eat in the classroom for a lunchtime social. This allows me to learn some of their interests.

Among classmates

Cooperative learning activities

Peer editing

Checking each other's work

Class jobs in pairs

Peer assisting and tutoring

Applause for each other

Show and tell

Homework buddies

Games

With parents

During the first week of school, I write a letter home to the parents to introduce myself, explain my class philosophy, and make them aware of my expectations of their children.

During the first month, I make phone calls to all parents.

At the beginning of a new unit, I send home a newsletter to parents to explain to them what we are studying.

I ask parents to send in anything they might have to enhance the unit or to come in to speak with the class.

I hold conferences with parents to discuss any concerns and achievements of students throughout the school year. These conferences might be initiated by me or the parents.

I send home weekly papers to inform parents of their child's progress. A behavior sheet for the week is attached to the papers, so parents are aware of good and bad behavior. These are signed and returned to ensure parents see them.

Strategies to develop student social skills

Conduct CMP mini-lessons to discuss appropriate and inappropriate behavior.

Students work with their classmates frequently to discuss ideas and complete assignments.

Provide opportunities for students to practice their best manners, such as Author Teas and Mother's Day/Father's Day luncheons.

Give Good Citizen badges to students.

Honor the Student of the Week.

Give "caught getting along" recognition.

Strategies to develop student problem-solving and decision-making skills

Have students work in pairs and small groups.

Give hands-on activities.

Allow students choices in projects.

Have students "Ask three before me."

Strategies to develop student self-control

Give praise for appropriate behavior.

Discuss why it is important to follow directions and behave.

Give behavior tickets.

Use self-monitoring charts and checks.

Preventive discipline strategies

Use eye contact and proximity.

Use positive reinforcement to encourage the ripple effect.

Use I-statements.

Monitor and mentor throughout lessons, moving around the room as I teach.

Use cues and signals.

Post class rules in a prominent location.

Practice "withitness."

Monitor continually.

Get to know students and what is going on in their lives.

Classroom technology plan

Technology is an important part of my classroom. Whenever possible, students work on computers. Computer lab time helps students become familiar with the different components of the computer. I implement age-appropriate software, both for research and pleasure. I publish student work on the computer and use e-mail for class pen pal projects.

EVALUATION

Grading Scheme

Students undergo evaluation in language arts, math, spelling, writing, social studies, and science. The types of grades assigned depend on the policy of the school system. Quizzes and homework receive a grade. Tests count double. Participation is averaged into the final grade. When report cards are issued, I hold a conference with every student about their grades and progress.

Recording grades in the grade book

I place grades in the grade book according to subject area. I record test grades in red and all others in black. I check off a row at the bottom of the grade book as I enter grades into the computer. Students are assigned a number for easier recording and filing purposes.

Homework policy

Students write homework in a composition book every day. It is the students' responsibility to bring their composition book to and from school every day. Unless certain circumstances arise, students have one assignment a day that takes approximately 20 to 30 minutes. I check homework the following day but do not grade it since assistance is usually given in the lower grades. Students who do not turn in homework in a timely fashion make it up in the classroom and make up missed homework during free time in the room. Students receive a weekly homework sheet with a list of assignments.

Progress reports

I issue progress reports in accordance with the district policy. Students and parents are able to assess progress through the weekly papers sent home.

Student opportunities to impact grades

Extra credit: *Yes, they have the opportunity to receive bonus points on tests or quizzes. Each subject has an extra credit folder that allows them to earn points toward their final grade.*

Rewrites: *No*

Drop a grade: *Possibly. I drop a grade only if the majority of the class does poorly, then review and retest.*

Special Assignments: *Yes*

Collection of points factored into final grade: *Yes, students receive points for cooperative learning activities and homework.*

PROFESSIONAL DEVELOPMENT

Reflection time is essential for teachers to collect their ideas on the day's events as well as plan for the days to come. On Thursdays, I eat lunch in my room and reflect on my teaching and the students' learning. I use the drive to and from school to reflect on my effectiveness at school. All teachers of my grade level stay at school each Monday after school to plan the week's lessons together.

SAMPLE PLAN 2

SAMPLE CMP FOR INTERMEDIATE GRADES

My Personal Classroom Management Plan

Grade Level: *Intermediate*

Teaching Goal: *Every child deserves a caring, enthusiastic, knowledgeable teacher who makes learning exciting, challenging, and fun.*

CLASSROOM ORGANIZATION

Classroom Environment
Draw or describe room arrangement

Figure 8.3

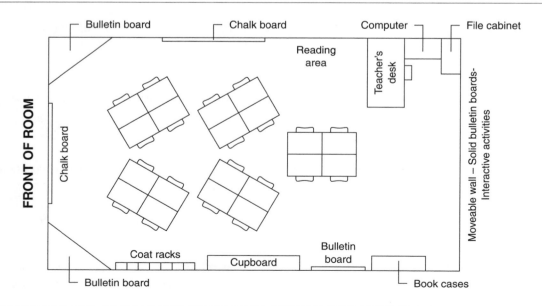

Sketch bulletin board ideas.

Students make autumn leaves out of construction paper, and write their names on them. We label the board "Fall Into Learning." The leaves also work well as a door decoration (Figure 8.4).

Figure 8.4

Class motto

(We say this each morning after the pledge of allegiance.)

I believe I can be a good student.

I believe I can achieve.

I believe that if I work hard, I will succeed.

Therefore, I will work hard each day to do my best.

I can learn.

I will learn! (Boyer 1995, p. 19)

Classroom Operation

Rules

Follow directions.

One person speaks at a time.

Mind your own business.

Keep feet, hands, and objects to yourself.

Use encouraging words.

Routines and procedures

I greet students at the door with a handshake and a warm greeting, and sometimes the "helper" helps me greet them. Upon entering the classroom in the morning, students take their magnetic name strip off the blackboard and put it on a chart indicating their lunch choice, which helps do lunch count and attendance quickly. Students write in their journals every morning. A teacher read-aloud occurs daily right after lunch recess to calm students down and prepare them for the afternoon.

"Specials" are scheduled daily for one hour and include art, physical education, music, library, computer lab.

Music plays in the morning while students prepare for the day and also sometimes during free reading and writing times.

Two wooden bathroom passes are on hooks, and when needed, students take a pass and put it on their desk, use the restroom, and return quickly. They can't leave the room if I am doing directed teaching unless it is an emergency.

Students may sharpen pencils as needed except during directed teaching.

After the routine is firmly established, a student helper has a stamp pad and stamp and helps fill out the Bingo sheets (see below) by collecting homework and stamping.

Students have a plan book in which they write down each assignment. They copy homework assignments and highlight them. The plan book goes home daily, and parents are asked to look for highlighted areas. Parents sign the plan book on weekends, unless a student has a problem with responsibility, in which case the plan book gets signed nightly.

Students have a folder with inside pockets. One pocket is labeled HOMEWORK, another is GRADED PAPERS, and a third is INFORMATION. Students keep the folder on their desk all day, and organize handouts as they arrive. This folder goes home each night and is to be returned each morning.

Consequences

Nonverbal reminder

Verbal reminder

Time-out: 15 minutes in classroom; fill out think sheet for parent signature.

Time-out: 30 minutes in another classroom; fill out think sheet for parent signature.

Severe clause: referral to the principal's office.

Incentives

Verbal incentives

Positive notes

Phone calls

Extra privileges

Projects

Certificates

Recesses

Free reading

Happy face stamp on hand, notebook, or index card on desks

Computer time

Teach a short lesson (supervised)

Individual incentives: Students begin each month with a Bingo sheet with 20 squares. They receive stamps for returning homework and notes or when "caught being good." When the sheet is filled, they draw out of a basket a cut-out on which is written an award, which is one of the incentives above. Students can fill more than one Bingo sheet each month.

Group incentives: Sometimes we do table points for rewards. Also, I use a time bank: I put minutes in a bank on the board when they cooperate and save minutes—30 minutes earns a recess.

On the wall in large letters is the word CATCHING. At the beginning of the school year I pass out letters that spell COMPLIMENTS. Students work in pairs decorating the letters (ownership). I laminate them and put them in a large envelope under the words CATCHING. When the whole class receives a compliment from another teacher, playground aides, or other staff, we post a letter until COMPLIMENTS is spelled out. Then we have a special class party, and start the process all over again.

Cues

Bell signal

Finger to the lips

Wink

Head shake

Frown

Smile

Snap fingers

Clap hands

Count down—5, 4, 3, 2, 1

INSTRUCTION

Lessons

Instructional strategies

Cooperative learning groups: One way I select cooperative groups is to distribute colored sticks, and students silently match colors to form new groups. I use a variety of ways to divide students into groups:

> *Pair-share*
>
> *Team-pair-solo: Students read and do activity or problem as a whole group or team (teach new concept, for example), then divide into pairs and do further work on the activity or problem with more details. For the solo portion, they must answer the problem or question to show understanding of the concept.*

Study guides

Journal writing: responses and explanations used in math, science, and social studies

Projects

Scoring guides

Alternate activities

Hands-on activities within lesson when possible

Thematic units

Skits and plays

Experiments, field trips, guest speakers, films, videos, or projects to strengthen skills or concepts taught

Create fun openers to lessons.

Focus students' attention on objectives of the lesson.

Give clear, step-by-step instructions, and always practice give-and-get in direction giving.

Always close a lesson using questioning techniques relating back to the lesson objective(s).

Make learning fun and find purpose in all learning.

Individualized instructional strategies

In some cases, give students pretests, and if they receive 95 percent or higher, they may do alternate activities.

Let students choose some of their own spelling words.

Let students do "Invent your own homework." They choose their own activity to work on and share with the class.

Use activities—bulletin boards, centers, brain busters—that foster individualized learning.

Use the tic-tac-toe format: Different activities appear on a form (standard tic-tac-toe grid) at different levels of Bloom's Taxonomy after a theme or unit of study. Students sign a contract for what they will complete—two tic-tac-toe rows (diagonal, horizontal, or vertical) for an A and so on. Students select activities.

Use portfolios and student assessments to build success.

Have students sign contracts whenever possible to hold them accountable for their learning.

Always be enthusiastic—give praise, positive comments, and handshakes, and smile often!

Assessment strategies

Walk around—never sitting at my desk.

Monitor and record individual progress on paper.

Board work

Questioning strategies

Just recalling knowledge

Comprehension questions

Probing and extending

Examples of questions

What is the author's purpose?

Give an example of fact and opinion statements.

Should Peter have acted the way he did when Fudge scribbled on his project?

Responses to students

When a student gives a correct answer:

Validate the answer.

Don't repeat it; have another student repeat the answer and tell why it is correct.

When a student gives a partially correct answer:

Use the information given and reword the question.

Turn to a partner and see if he or she can give rest of answer.

Let students talk it over and have the first student then give correct answer.

When a student gives an incorrect answer:

Say "That's the answer to another question I was thinking of—way to go!"

"Now, listen again as I ask the original question," then reword the question.

"Talk to your Study Buddy and see if the two of you can figure out the answer."

"Listen to your friend answer the question, then I want you to repeat the answer."

Always dignify their answer, but hold them accountable.

Student self-evaluation opportunities

At the end of each project/presentation, students receive a form (tailored to each) on which they evaluate their effort, quality of work, and so on. I fill one out also, and we have a conference on the forms.

Students receive a blank report card (before I send it home), evaluate their work, and make comments.

They set goals each quarter, and write an evaluation at the end of the quarter (which goes into the report card envelope) stating whether they met their goal and explaining why or why not.

Students graph their progress on assignments, quizzes, and so on.

Effective Teaching Practices
Building positive relationships
Between teacher and students

Make announcements on the intercom about successes in the room.

Greet students at the door each morning either with a handshake or brief comments. At night I walk them to the bus and give them another handshake or pat and brief wishes for a good evening.

Eat lunch with students in the classroom and sometimes in the cafeteria.

Dialogue in journals; I comment on their entries, and ask and answer questions.

Give them notes, happy grams, stickers.

Among classmates

Group work

Buddy system

Peer tutoring

Desk clusters

Group names

Catch them complimenting or encouraging each other.

With parents

Phone calls to parents about student successes

Weekly class-written newsletter

Notes in student plan books

Invitations to project presentations

Open-door policy in the classroom

Introductory letter

Strategies to develop student social skills

Our school has a program to develop social skills called Responsibility, Effort, Solving problems, Perseverance, Empathy, Cooperation, and Teamwork (RESPECT). The skills are introduced on the intercom by groups of students through raps, poems, and other ways. Each teacher follows up in his or her own classroom by using literature, games, writing activities, and so on.

Fourth graders and fifth graders meet on a regular basis to do fun activities such as reading and writing.

Hold class meetings to build teamwork, plan activities, and solve conflicts.

Strategies to develop student problem-solving and decision-making skills

Students always are problem solving, from formal math to brain teasers.

Use interactive bulletin boards.

Solve class problems with class meetings.

Complete assessment tasks for new Missouri Assessment Project (MAP).

Use contracts: students decide what grades they want to make and decide upon activities, projects, presentations.

Use portfolios: students select which work goes into them and why.

Students earn and decide upon reward parties and do all the planning and organizing for them.

At times, students choose which literature book and group they wish to work in. They decide who they want to sit next to at assemblies. I remind them of class expectations, then they choose.

Strategies to develop student self-control

Use the restroom when needed: two passes hang on magnets; students take a pass and put it on their desk, and when they return to the room, they hang the pass back up.

Sharpen pencils when needed.

Use any and all of teacher's supplies and manipulatives as needed.

Move around room as needed.

Allow students to select their "Quality Papers" for portfolio.

Always give students choices.

Preventive discipline strategies

Nonverbals

Body language

Eye contact

Proximity

Touching on shoulder, head, or hand

Classroom technology plan

Students attend computer lab twice a week for 30-minute periods. They use the Internet, Encarta, and various software.

EVALUATION

Grading Scheme

Tests count twice. Projects count as tests. Points are collected for group work.

Recording grades in the grade book

I write the assignment title plus the percentage grade in the grade book. I draw a box around late and missing assignments and put in the grade when students complete the assignment. I can tell at a glance which students have poor study skills.

Homework policy

Our homework policy is a well-defined policy outlined in detail to students and parents at the beginning of the school year. It requires parents', students', and teacher's signatures. Briefly, five late assignments (i.e., not ready by 8:45 A.M.) result in an afterschool detention. After the detention, students start over with a clean slate. Each quarter, late assignments are erased and each student starts with zero demerits.

Progress reports

Progress reports are called "mid-quarters," and each student receives one halfway through the quarter. The form allows for percentage grades for each subject and comments and suggestions for remediation if necessary. This form requires a parental signature so "no surprises" occur at report card time.

Student opportunities to impact grades

Extra credit: *Yes*

Rewrites: *Yes*

Drop a grade: *No*

Special assignments: *Yes*

Collection of points to be factored into the final grade: *No*

Professional development

There seems to be no time during school. After school, I often reflect on lessons that went well or didn't go as well as I expected. I make notes on the lesson plans or in the teacher's guide. I spend evenings on reflections and make changes in the next day's lesson plans. Approximately once a month, our regularly scheduled faculty meeting is devoted to professional development. In addition, three day-long teacher inservice programs are scheduled per year.

SAMPLE PLAN 3

SAMPLE CMP FOR MIDDLE GRADES

My Personal Classroom Management Plan

Grade Level: *Middle*

Teaching Goal: *Leave the classroom better than I found it!*

CLASSROOM ORGANIZATION

Classroom Environment

Draw or describe room arrangement

My classroom looks like a traditional classroom for the first four or five weeks; however, after I start the cooperative learning groups the classroom changes. Seats are assigned by learning groups, as indicated by broken lines in Figure 8.5, and set up in a semicircle around the front of the room. Each of the four corners of the room fulfills an important role in helping me teach. One corner acts as a time-out center. The second corner is a reward-type "living room" with easy chairs and rugs. The third is a computer center, and the last corner contains a large table and bookcase and functions as a book/reading/meeting place.

Figure 8.5

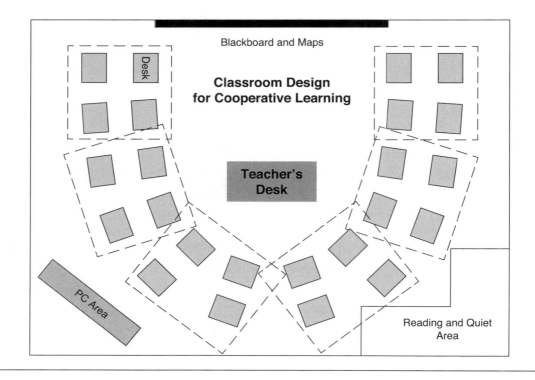

Sketch bulletin board ideas

The February "Famous Americans" unit highlights a person of the day. A picture of the person and a description strip are added to the board and discussed (see Figure 8.6).

Figure 8.6

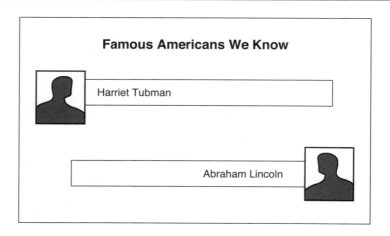

Class motto

We are all in this together!

Knowledge is power!

Classroom Operation

Rules

Be prepared.

Be respectful to everyone.

Be responsible.

Participate in class activities.

Obey all school rules.

Routines and procedures

Students are to sharpen pencils when they arrive in the classroom, before the bell rings. Once class starts, I cover the sharpener with an old sock. They then know not to approach the sharpener and not to ask to sharpen their pencil. For those who miss the chance, I have an "out" can with sharpened pencils they can borrow and an "in" can for unsharpened pencils.

All class work and homework assignments are numbered and posted in the classroom. Students who miss a day of school do not ask me what they missed; instead, they take responsibility and copy the missed assignments from the chart.

I or any student can call a class meeting to talk about rule violations or any other problem. The procedure is to place a note in the basket asking for a meeting the next day. The class meeting supports classroom participation and teaches problem solving.

Students section their three-ring notebook by subject. Each section has a table of contents listing assigned work, my letter to the parents stating my grading policy, and a parent review sheet. All assignments are numbered and returned to students for them to place them in the notebook in order. Parents can review the notebook any time and identify any missing assignments by means of the numbering. It is the student's responsibility to keep the notebook updated; however, I perform notebook checks routinely.

The class establishes cooperative learning rules, creates procedures, and shares expectations to aid the efficiency, effectiveness, and productivity of students when working in cooperative learning groups. I provide specific and simple directions either through handouts or by writing them on the chalkboard. I teach each step and ask students to summarize the directions. I establish cues that tell students to focus attention on me. I set a time limit for each step in the process, give the cue for students to enter their groups, and then I circulate and monitor group progress.

Every week, I take the classroom climate, which tells me how students rate the learning environment of the past week. Students turn in a climate sheet without a name so they can comment without fear. They rate the environment on a scale of 1 to 10, with 1 being poor and 10, the best. They also tell me what they liked and disliked about the past week's instruction. Each Monday morning, after they turn in homework, we discuss the previous week's climate sheets. This routine gets students involved in the class, provides me with feedback, and allows me to point out behaviors that either help or hinder the class.

Tuesday through Friday morning routine is that students turn in homework and write in journals for 5 to 10 minutes on the most important lesson(s) they learned the day before, either in or out of school.

Each day has an ending routine; closure activities of the day include writing homework assignments, discussing the day's lessons and, if earned, free talk time.

Consequences (in order of implementation)

Logical consequences:

Those in which students must make right what they have done wrong

If they make a mess, they clean it.

If they willfully damage material, they must replace it.

Generic consequences:

Nonverbal cues including eye contact, proximity, and body language/hand signal

Verbal cues including use of student's name, I-statement, signal words, i.e., "Stop," "Check yourself," or words students select to signal inappropriate behavior

Conventional consequences:

Time out where student goes to assigned place either in or out of the classroom during student's free time (lunch time, time between classes, etc.)

Conference with student during student's free time:

Written conduct notice or telephone conference with parent and/or school detention

In-school parent conference

Visit with principal

In-school suspension, suspension

Incentives

Group incentives:

"Talk time" during class time

Class parties

Freedom Fridays

Individual incentives:

Homework passes

Point coupons, worth points for graded assignments

Free time for library use and activities centers

Overtime reward certificate placed on the bulletin board when I "catch" a student putting in more than 100% effort

Cues

Counting backward from 5

Raising a hand and moving to the front of the room

Turning the lights on and off

Crossing my arms and tapping my foot in front of the class

A whistle, bell, or chime

INSTRUCTION

Lessons

Instructional strategies

I believe an active classroom supports greater learning. My teaching strategy for the first four to five weeks of the school year is a traditional teaching manner, with enough activity to keep students from getting bored. This allows me to establish credibility as a teacher, teach the social skills and rules, and gather information on students' abilities.

After I have all the information I need and I have established myself, we move into cooperative learning groups. I feel the use of cooperative learning has many advantages over traditional methods, including greater use of higher-level reasoning, more on-task behavior, increased motivation, persistence in completing tasks, and better general attitudes toward school.

Enrichment of student learning is a powerful tool. Field trips, guest speakers, videotapes, and other resources provide students with a real, "live" look at where their education can take them and possible goals for their future.

Assessment strategies

Quick Writes

Cues—such as pencils down when work is completed

Use checks for understanding—All stand if this is the answer

Give examples and ask for agreement

Questioning strategies

Use higher-level questioning.

Have students write questions instead of answers.

Use Bloom's Taxonomy to formulate questions.

Prompt, probe for answers.

Use piggyback questioning.

Ask "Why?"

Examples of questions

Why do you think that happened?

Persuade me to choose that product.

Responses to students

When a student gives a correct answer:

"Exactly!"

"Absolutely."

"You got that right!"

"Yea!"

Silent clap

Thumbs up

When a student gives a partially correct answer:

"Keep going."

"Add some more ideas."

"Think about this; now tell me what you think."

When a student gives an incorrect answer:

"Whoa, slow down. Let's get some more facts!"

"Let's discuss this more, then return to that question."

"Scratch that for now!"

Student self-evaluation opportunities

Check their work.

Exchange papers.

Use the answer sheet.

Use portfolios.

Graph progress.

Keep a progress folder.

Perform self-evaluation inventories.

Effective Teaching Practices

Building positive relationships

Between teacher and student

Help sessions

Greeting students at the door

Class climate surveys

Agendas and schedules

Among classmates

Classroom buddy system

Information scavenger hunt about students

Interview other students and share the information

Student spotlight

Student mentoring and tutoring

Cooperative learning

Conflict resolution role-playing

With parents

Have parents act as guest speakers.

Class-written newsletters

Telephone calls

Notes

Strategies to develop social skills

Students design a name plate they feel represents them, then explain their design to the class.

A pair of students interviews and introduces each other to the class.

The class participates in a scavenger hunt to find out information about classmates such as, Who has a pet? Who likes baseball?

Teach and model good social skills.

Teach how to get into and work in groups, how to talk to each other, and how to display respect, and teach conflict management skills.

Observe groups as they perform activities and, specifically, look for evidence that students are practicing interpersonal/social skills. Give feedback and reinforcement to the groups using these skills.

Strategies to develop student problem-solving and decision-making skills

Improved problem-solving and decision-making abilities are two major benefits of cooperative learning. The ability to solve problems requires many of the social skills students must learn to be effective at establishing relationships and at collaborative learning. As a group, students must decide how to pursue whatever task they have been assigned or even pick the assignment themselves. I believe the motivation, persistence, and higher-level reasoning skills used in cooperative learning are the same as those used in decision making. By putting students into situations where they must use these skills, we teach decision making. In addition, I teach problem-solving and decision-making skills by means of CMP mini-lessons.

Strategies to develop student self-control

Conflict resolution strategies

Peer resolution

Peer mediating

Contracts

Preventive discipline strategies

Behavior modification involves the general use of positive and logical consequences to change student behavior. As a rule I do not use punishment, or negative reinforcers, because they prove less effective. The method I use involves identifying the behaviors that are to receive special attention and deciding which of the four positive reinforcers—social, graphic, activity, or tangible—to use.

First and foremost, I teach the class rules, incentives, and consequences. Other strategies include use of contracts between students and me and providing routines for the day-to-day operation of the classroom. My goal is to foster a sense of togetherness by regularly talking with the class about what they can accomplish as a group and teaching them how to deal with problems they encounter.

Classroom technology plan

My class uses computers. Software is acquired to supplement class learning. I also use videotapes, CD-ROMs, and the Internet. The computer lab is used for writing assignments and skills practice. The class corresponds with another middle school class in another state via e-mail.

EVALUATION

Grading Scheme

I use the grading scale of the school system in which I teach. I believe students' time and effort are important to include in the grade. Because of this, every item of work students turn in has some point value, and the student receives feedback. This allows students to bring up their point level and shows them that everything they turn in is important to me and has value. Tests count twice as much as assignments.

Recording grades in the grade book

Each student receives a number that coincides with his or her placement in the grade book. Students write this number next to their name on all completed work.

Homework policy

Homework reinforces the day's lessons. My policy is to assign no more than an hour of homework Monday through Thursday, with no homework on Fridays for the weekend. The routine for turning in homework and other collectable work is as follows: Each learning group has a manager. The manager collects the work from the group members and turns it over to the class manager who, with the help of the assistant manager, places the collected work in student number order.

Progress reports

Progress reports are issued as the school system requires.

Student opportunities to impact grades

Extra credit opportunities: *I believe effort is important, and I provide opportunities for students to improve their grade by doing extra credit work. Also, students receive extra credit points for returning forms the next day and for bringing parents into the classroom as volunteers or for getting parents to attend Open House, conferences, and so on.*

Rewrite opportunities: *Students may rewrite some assignments, but the rewrite is averaged with the first grade to get a new grade. For example, a student writes a paper, receives a "C," and asks for a rewrite. The rewritten paper receives an "A." When the two grades are averaged, the paper receives a "B."*

Drop a grade: *When all homework has a point value and students are allowed to rewrite assignments, the need to drop grades does not come up.*

Point system: *Each question, or problem, in an assignment has a point value. The points are arranged on a continuum with a range of points assigned a letter grade. At predetermined times in the school marking period, I divide the total number of points the student earns, including extra credit, by the maximum total possible points, excluding the extra credit work, to determine a percentage that corresponds with a letter grade on the continuum.*

PROFESSIONAL DEVELOPMENT

Over the years, I have found only two ways to improve at anything: First, ask those with more knowledge or skills to show me how it's done. I ask teachers who I feel have a complementary style to help teach me what I need to know. Second, I read every publication or book I can that contains useful information to take to the classroom.

Teaming in the middle school provides an extra planning bell that gives teachers time to meet together and plan lessons. We discuss certain students, situations, and problems. We reflect on our role in the students' success or failure.

SAMPLE CMPs FOR SECONDARY GRADES

My Personal Classroom Management Plan

Grade Level: *Secondary*

Teaching Goal: *Make it relevant. Make it worth learning. Make it impossible to forget!*

CLASSROOM ORGANIZATION

Classroom Environment

Draw or describe room arrangement

> *All desks face the room's center to generate an open forum of discussion, action, and sharing (see Figure 8.7).*

Figure 8.7

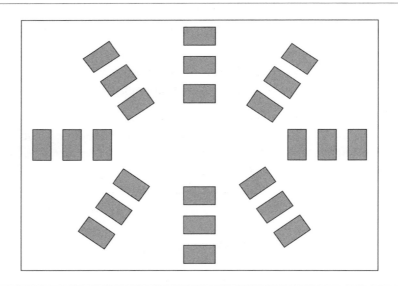

Sketch bulletin board ideas

> *See Figure 8.8. Under "Past," there might be a news story or other document pertaining to the 1960s civil rights movement. "Today" might highlight a current news story describing the continued struggle for human rights and racial harmony. Under "Tomorrow," I post student essays reflecting student opinions, insights, and solutions on the topic of human rights.*

Figure 8.8

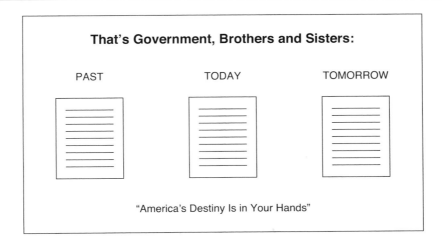

Class motto

What you lack is experience, not intelligence!

America's destiny is in your hands!

If you don't like it, work to make it better!

Classroom Operation

Rules

Respect yourself.

Respect others.

Respect this class.

Routines and procedures

Political cartoon for discussion

Teacher reading of a famous quote or a page or two from a novel featuring a theme or message that parallels the content of the day's lesson

Consequences

Warning

Stern eye contact

Hand gestures

Hall conference

Phone call to a parent and a parent conference

Incentives

>*High fives*
>
>*Opportunities such as "Letters to the Editor"*
>
>*Coronation into the Writers' Guild*
>
>*Sodas and Walkmans placed into the regular routine of the day*

Cues

>*Hand raised*
>
>*Eye contact*
>
>*Saying, "Ladies and Gentlemen."*
>
>*Waving my hand a certain way means "I'll get to you later," "Move over there," and "Stop [a particular activity]."*
>
>*Touch a shoulder or desk so student ends the action deemed inappropriate.*

INSTRUCTION

Lessons

Instructional strategies

>*Mix lecture with discussion, debate, research, writing, and role-playing.*
>
>*Plan active student involvement in lessons with questions, board work, hands-on activities, and group work.*
>
>*Foster participation through comments, concerns, opinions, and criticisms.*
>
>*Provide demonstrations.*
>
>*Provide purpose for learning material.*
>
>*Dare to be different.*
>
>*Plan materials to interest students.*

Individualized instructional strategies

>*Offer multiple assignments.*
>
>*Offer multiple ways of completing assignments.*
>
>*I have always treated all my students—"at-risk," "average," and "gifted"— as individuals. Each student possesses special talents that can compensate for weaknesses. For example, I offer oral tests if a student does not do well on written exams. If a student cannot write a letter to the editor, he or she can draw a political cartoon or give an oral presentation. The course is tailored to meet students' needs.*

Assessment strategies

Notebook activities

Questions and answers—Do you agree with _____?

Put information in your "own" words.

Questioning strategies

First ask who, what, where, and when. Then ask why, how, and what are your perceptions.

Play devil's advocate.

Examples of questions

If the U.S. history topic is Manifest Destiny, I ask someone to define it, tell when and where it occurred, and who was involved. Then I ask, What was the intent of Manifest Destiny, why was it so eagerly embraced, and was it cruel? What was accomplished? How were people helped? How were lives and cultures ruined? Next, I ask, if you were a white pioneer during the period, would you have done differently or would you, too, have become a participant? How can one judge the past fairly? Does America owe anyone an apology? Are we different today?

Responses to students

When a student gives a correct answer:

"Right on!"

"Hey, you're so smart, you should be the teacher!"

"I told you that you could do it!"

"You're the greatest!"

"Yea!"

When a student gives a partially correct answer:

I approach the desk of the student, get down on my knees, and say, "Add a little more."

"Go on!"

Ask the class to help us out.

When a student gives an incorrect answer:

"Keep on trying!"

Provide a hint.

Solicit help from the class.

Student self-evaluation opportunities

Graph grades.

Comment on progress.

Effective Teaching Practices

Building positive relationships

Between teacher and students

Let students know I want to be here teaching.

Accept/promote student opinions and uniqueness.

Listen to their concerns.

Get to know them.

Be there for them.

Be honest.

Among classmates

Require students to listen to each other.

Accept opinions.

Be sensitive to cultural and individual differences.

Be polite.

"Catch" them being kind to each other.

With parents

Be honest.

Be firm.

Be compassionate.

Show interest in their child.

Strategies to develop student social skills

Model desired behavior.

Don't preach, but simply offer a reason to behave differently.

Strategies to develop student problem-solving
and decision-making skills

Get student input.

Allow students to make choices and decisions.

Ask the student what he or she could/should have done.

Strategies to develop student self-control

It begins with the speech, "You will not always have a teacher, preacher, or parent standing before you; consequently, you must learn to accept accountability and develop a healthy sense of self-discipline."

Share examples of self-discipline.

Celebrate student examples of self-discipline.

Preventive discipline strategies

Emphasize the positive.

Be respectful.

Set high expectations.

Be enthusiastic.

Be knowledgeable in the subject matter.

Handle problems immediately.

Classroom technology plan

Use the Internet for research.

Use e-mail for correspondence.

Use the VCR for tapes.

EVALUATION

Grading scheme

I strive to have four recorded grades per week. A minimum of two are quizzes. Tests, papers, projects, and oral presentations represent the rest.

Recording grades in the grade book

All assignments are graded in green ink, never red.

Color-code the grade book: green ink = test; black ink = quiz; purple ink = project

Homework policy

I give homework assignments to prepare students better for a quiz or test. A low grade usually reflects a student's failure to complete the assignment. Some essay questions are initiated or completed at home; failure to submit an essay can leave a negative impression on one's overall average. I am opposed to teacher policies that use homework as a major element in averaging grades.

Progress reports

Students receive progress reports during each grading period.

Student opportunities to impact grades

Extra credit: *Yes*

Rewrites: *Yes*

Drop a grade: *Maybe*

Special assignments: *Yes*

Collection of points to be factored into the final grade: *Maybe*

Professional development

I spend time reflecting on the highs and lows of the day and formulate strate-gies to eliminate the lows and maintain the highs. This time usually takes place as I drive from school to my second job. A couple times a year, the faculty/staff participate in inservice training. I try to attend a professional conference every two years. I take one or two college courses every five years for recertification.

Managing classroom behavior may be more challenging today than ever before. Teachers face daily the major concerns facing public education: larger class sizes, lack of discipline, use of drugs, more fighting, violence, gangs, and more diversity in students' abilities and cultures. As Barbetta, Norona, and Bicard (2005) report, "Teachers are challenged daily to create and maintain a positive, productive classroom atmosphere conducive to learning" (p. 11). The first step in meeting this challenge is in developing and implementing a personal class-room management plan.

SAMPLE PLAN 5

My Personal Classroom Management Plan

Grade Level: *Secondary*

Teaching Goal: *I will engage my students so that we all become a part of the active learning process and have some fun in doing so. This will be a social stud-ies classroom that they will remember.*

CLASSROOM ORGANIZATION

Classroom Environment

Draw or describe room arrangement

The desks are arranged in two semicircles, one inside the other, so that everyone has a clear view while discussions are going on. It is a bit of a modified Socratic dialogue setup. A stool moves about the horseshoe for me to perch on. We have a book and magazine resource area that has a table and a couple of "thinking chairs." Magazine subscriptions, such as Smithsonian *or* Time, *will help everyone to stay in touch with current events and figures. There will be bulletin boards on either side of the blackboard. One will be used to display our class agreement, or social contract, and assignment reminders. The second will dis-play school rules and procedures. There is another large bulletin board in the back of the room, which I call the "Wall of Fame." This one is used to display test results, achievement awards, class motto, and SOL (Standards of Learning) progress (where we are in the course). There is an area on the board at the front of the room with magnetic clips so that students may display upcoming school events that they are involved in and wish to announce to the class. There are also a couple of dry erase boards for larger group-work situations in the two back corners of the room. My desk is at the back of the room, so that I have a clear view of what is going on. In addition, there will be various inspiring posters, geographical maps, and nation flags all over the room.*

Provide rough draft or sketch of bulletin board ideas

Figure 8.9

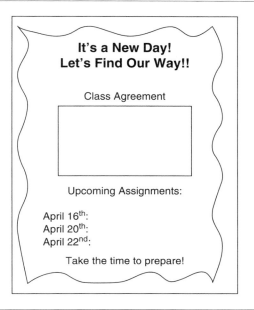

Class motto

Learn to Understand . . . Understand to Learn!

Classroom Operation

Rules

Respect yourself and those around you.

Do not be rude.

Bring it! ☺

Though the list is short, these are broad rules that can be applied to many classroom issues. Students have fewer rules to remember. Since these are umbrella-type rules, the students hold more responsibility to consider the appropriateness of their comments and actions prior to making them.

Routines and procedures

At the beginning of the school year, or semester, the class participates in an exercise led by me to help them establish the rules and expectations of group work tasks.

This allows them the opportunity to participate in the structure of the activities. I will be looking for suggestions such as respect, responsibility, participation, organization, role-taking, and good listening and communication skills. After making suggestions as to the qualities of an effective team, this list then becomes the guideline for cooperative learning experiences. These will then be displayed on our bulletin board as our "Class Agreement." I will distribute laminated copies for the students' binder and send a copy home for parents to review.

In addition, I will also outline my expectations for their behavior during the course of the year. We will discuss ideas such as responsibilities, respect, timeliness, and consequences. In addition, I will add to the conversation what they can expect from me in regards to timely feedback, grading systems, extra credit opportunities, and assistance outside of the classroom.

Note-taking skills will be a focus during the first few weeks of class. This skill will be very important during their academic years.

As class begins each day, students will jot down the objectives for the day as noted on the upper right-hand corner of the chalkboard. They will do so in their notebook that is designated for this course.

On a daily basis, if the directions for the day's activities are verbal, I will ask students to recall them for me. This way I am able to determine whether there is a clear understanding or if there is a need for further explanation. If the activity involves written directions, the students will be given the necessary time to read the instructions and then a brief question-and-answer period will follow.

I will be mindful during discussion sessions to allow sufficient response time, as well as to call on a variety of students. I will use a laminated seating chart and a grease pencil as tools to assist in keeping track of whom I have called on. In many situations, if the student I call upon is unable to answer, rather than immediately opening the question up to the rest of the class, I may offer additional information to help provide the student with cues.

Each class has its own tray that stays on our bookshelves. Any homework is turned in as the students enter the classroom.

The class syllabus is kept in the front of their three-ring binders so that it is easily accessible for reference or adjustments.

Handouts are distributed with holes already punched in them so that students may place them in their notebooks with ease. This is also a tool to help them maintain their study resources.

Weekly feedback will take place on Fridays toward the end of the class time. We are able to establish a routine and an open line of communication this way. The chosen tool, such as an exit card or a feedback grid, will be returned on Mondays at the beginning of class time.

On days that students are participating in cooperative learning activities, groups that complete their assignment early may take that spare time to use our reading area, team study, or add an entry to their journal.

Self-evaluation assessments will also be used periodically to aid both the student's and my own ability to determine areas that may need additional focus.

Each class session ends with a summary of the day's objectives, a reminder of the next day's assignment and homework, and an open-floor question opportunity.

Consequences

Nonverbal recognition of undesired behavior (hand or facial gesture, body language, etc.)

Verbal request for a behavioral change

Final verbal reminder

An individual discussion in private

Parents contacted

Incentives

Verbal praise

Free time in the reading area

Democratic selection between two activities for the day

Cues

Class is aware that when I flash them the peace symbol I am requesting quiet— Peace and Quiet.

Raise right hand and say, "Right here please."

Tap on desk/chalkboard.

"Let's refocus for a moment."

A code word of choice

Tonality

A rain stick as a noisemaker to regain attention

INSTRUCTION

Lessons

Instructional strategies

My intention is to create an environment in which students are comfortable, both physically and emotionally, and feel confident in their role as active learners. It is necessary to build the students' skills in order for them to become thoroughly involved in the process. To do so, we will commit some of our initial time together to learning to understand how we may assure our success throughout the year. It is to our advantage to become familiar with one another. I plan to use some icebreaking strategies in the early days of our meetings. I want the students to have an opportunity to get to know each other, as well as for me to get to know each of them. A variety of student assessments, such as personal inventories, will aid me in assuring that I am sufficiently differentiating my instruction in the future. Having an understanding of each of my students will also assist me to vary my teaching methods sufficiently in order to effectively reach Gardner's Multiple Intelligences, the varied learning modalities, and to incorporate cooperative learning into my lessons. In addition, we will focus on skills such as note taking, creating foldables, research, writing, and a variety of others to enhance the students' experiences.

Once we have established ground rules and a rapport, we can then ease our way into effective cooperative learning situations. I plan to use many different approaches to group work, including paired sharing, short-term teams, and project teams. Care should be taken in assigning groups so that diversity can provide students the opportunity to experience varying opinions and choices. These group tasks help to better prepare students for real-world experiences.

I also believe that lecture sessions are necessary. However, I do not feel that they must strictly adhere to traditional methods of delivery. I am especially fond of participating in a Socratic dialogue format. It is a circular manner of organized, seated discussion, which is led by an individual who moves about the center of the circle. This is the reasoning behind my choice of classroom environment earlier in this plan. It can be a wonderful way to begin class on a day that the students had a homework assignment that involved reading a certain selection from their textbooks. It encourages many positives such as eye contact, polite communication, excitement for the content, and many more. Students will become excited about the process as an extension of my zeal.

Many strategies will be used in the classroom in order to differentiate instruction. I desire to reach out to each style of learner in my classroom. Graphic organizers, practice time, media presentations, and real-life examples are all ways to pursue varying my teaching techniques in order to reach all of my students. Application can be especially powerful. I plan to provide real-world scenarios as often as possible; this is especially applicable in the social studies classroom.

I also consider it important to help students understand what to expect. I can build on this belief by providing them with class-time review sessions and study guides prior to delivery of a graded assessment. In addition, I will be available for remedial time after school to help students. Primarily, I want to be certain to make myself both accessible and approachable. I also plan to be active in school activities that go on outside of my classroom. I want students to see me at the pep rallies, the assemblies, and the basketball games, and know that I will be there to cheer them on. I plan to have "withitness." I want to work hard to let my students know that I am here to help them be successful.

Individualized instructional strategies

Reflecting on using assessment tools at the beginning of the school year, individual student interest surveys are beneficial toward becoming acquainted with each student. In addition, just taking the time to talk with them during spare moments helps to build a bond and smooth the daily interactions. Developing a positive relationship with students helps them to feel safe and secure in my classroom.

They will then be more likely to feel comfortable enough to share ideas and participate in discussions. I hope to encourage my students to be confident enough to think outside the box when analyzing issues. It is important at this age level that we model good relationship habits.

In order to align with Gardner's Multiple Intelligence theory, I plan to occasionally offer a selection of activities for graded assessment purposes. For example, students may have a choice between turning in a written essay, creating a poster, or engaging in a paired debate in reference to a specific topic. This gives students the opportunity to govern themselves a bit.

I will also make myself available for independent or remedial study opportunities after school as needed.

Assessment strategies

Walk around and observe

Chart and record student information

Use many checks for understanding

Use Quick Writes

Note body language

Ask for examples

Provide many guided practice activities

Questioning strategies

Bloom's Taxonomy is an essential tool. We learn to start with recall as our foundation and build upward. In order to prepare our students for end-of-semester testing, we must put to use more than simple recall skills and yes-or-no questions. We must ask questions that require reasoning skills, and the abilities to compare and contrast, as well as to evaluate information.

Likewise, it is incredibly important to assure that we are involving each student and that we provide them with ample time to respond. A laminated seating chart will be helpful in tracking this. In the instance that a student is having difficulty responding to a question, I will try to add a bit more information to help cue him or her.

Examples of questions

Tell me why you think that might be the case.

Would you have done it the same way?

What would you do differently?

What are the two main contributing factors?

How are the two concepts connected?

What are the common characteristics?

How could there have been greater success?

Responses to Students

When a student gives a correct answer:

"Awesome!"

"Very true!"

"Good job!"

"You've got it!"

"Exactly!"

"Beautiful!"

"Bingo!"

"Absolutely!"

"You rock!"

"Fantastic!"

"Excellent!"

"Call her butter. She's on a roll!"

"True, true!"

When a student gives a partially correct answer:

"And why do you think that is so?"

"Can you expand on that?"

"Nice details. Tell me about . . . next time, too."

"Good start. Keep trying."

When a student gives an incorrect answer:

"Good try. Does anyone have anything to add?"

"Let's talk about that for a minute."

"But was that really why . . . ?"

"Maybe, but it was more of a . . . ?"

"Let's come back to that."

Cue them.

Student self-evaluation opportunities

Trade-n-grade

Personal inventory

Student-led parent conferences

Goal setting and graphing progress

Self-evaluation questionnaire

Comments on feedback

Written evaluation

Pre-assessment to a new unit

EFFECTIVE TEACHING PRACTICES

Building Positive Relationships

Between Teachers and Students

Be consistent.

Be fair.

Put notes at the top of assignments.

Listen to them and respond.

Give timely feedback.

Be genuine.

Have withitness—attend school social functions and important events.

Laugh—with them, at yourself, just do it!

Be positive.

Be understanding.

Create a safe environment for them.

Greet students at the door or in the hallway.

Be approachable.

Get acquainted with them as individuals.

Encourage them to be the version of them.

Be supportive.

Be knowledgeable.

Among Classmates

Cooperative learning

Role-playing situations

Paired activities

Group icebreakers at beginning of the year

Peer teaching

Jigsaw strategy

Encourage listening skills and sharing

Peer tutoring

Encourage extra-curricular activities

With Parents

Phone calls home at the beginning of the year

Send home a copy a class "Social Contract."

Be honest.

Be consistent.

Progress reports

Notes of praise sent home

Good communication

Strategies to develop student social skills

Icebreaker activities

Talk about effective ways to work together.

Strategically pair students for activities.

Change seating arrangements temporarily.

Discuss good communication and listening skills.

Sponsor a club.

Encourage extracurricular involvement.

Model good social skills with other professionals.

Strategies to develop student self-control

Sound classroom discipline from the beginning

Teach evaluative skills.

Talk about the concept.

Train students to be peer mediators.

Build inductive and deductive reasoning abilities.

Provide students with opportunities to do so.

Recognize and commend such actions.

Discuss expectations.

Student–teacher contracts

Share personal instances.

Preventive discipline strategies

Be fair and consistent.

Clearly understood consequences

Identify the behavior.

Explore alternate decisions the student could have made.

Class rules

Incentives

Model good behavior and cooperation.

Discuss what is expected of students.

Talk about good responses to situations.

Address quickly.

Classroom technology plan

PowerPoint presentations

Cable in the classroom

DVD viewing

Online research and in-class activities—Web Quest

Web-buddies

Computer software programs—Word, etc.

EVALUATION

Grading Scheme

Recording grades in the grade book

School districts set the primary grading scale. Fortunately, since I want to encourage different learning styles, I will have a variety of assignments to grade. I will assign at least two written, graded homework assignments each week. That way I can gauge students' efforts and comprehension. There will be at least one project-type assignment per unit, along with three cooperative tasks. In order to prepare for the next week, I plan to administer a map/graph quiz or a reading review on Fridays. At the conclusion of each unit, we will have a comprehensive graded assessment. My assessments will extend well beyond multiple-choice structure in order to reach out to the various styles of learners in my classroom. On written reports, I will allow students to complete a "rewrite" and average the two scores. Tests will carry the most weight. Homework will be graded cumulatively toward a set goal. Students' names will be recorded in the grade book alphabetically according to their last names. This allows for ease in entering data or finding information quickly.

Homework policy

Checking homework allows me to examine students' comprehension, as well as make an assessment of their growing reasoning skills. It can also offer a red flag if there happens to be a drastic change in performance that could be caught prior to their average being severely affected or if there is a concept that I may not have explained well enough to the group. We will have at least two written, graded homework assignments each week. Occasionally, we will trade-n-grade in order to encourage cooperative habits. These repetitive habits help to move information from short-term memory into long-term memory or from fluid to crystallized knowledge. Each class has an assigned tray on our bookshelves in the reading area for their homework. Students are to turn their assignments in when entering class. Points will be awarded for each assignment. These points are added up cumulatively toward a top score of 100, which is then a part of their overall course grade. No late assignments will be accepted.

Progress reports

The school district assigns formal dates for report card issuance. I also believe it can be helpful to send home notes of praise when students have made an especially strong effort or performed very well. It's a win–win situation. In the classroom, the students' grade-recording section in their notebooks will serve as a daily reminder of growth. Should a student's grades take a turn for the worse, I would contact the parents or guardians so we could design a plan to help the student get back on track.

Student opportunities to impact grades

Extra credit: *Might be offered a couple of times a semester, but not very often. In the real world, there are not often chances for "do-overs." I hope to aid in preparing my students for their lives beyond high school. If I contribute to a dependency on opportunities to take back or reform original efforts, I am lessening the likelihood of their success.*

Rewrites: *Available on papers. Results will be averaged.*

Drop a grade: *One quiz grade per semester*

Special assignments: *If required by an IEP. Otherwise, I am hoping to encourage responsibility in my students and special assignments have the potential to take away from that. However, in the unique case of a gifted student, I am more than willing to redesign materials to provide more of a challenge.*

PROFESSIONAL DEVELOPMENT

I will set aside at least 15 minutes each day to reflect on what went well and what needs improvement. I will make a plan to solve problems immediately. I plan to attend school inservice activities. I have made a commitment to my teaching by planning to observe an effective teacher in my school at least twice a year.

References

Alschuler, A. S. (1980). *School discipline: A socially literate solution.* New York: McGraw-Hill.

Ball, D. (2000). Bridging practices: Intertwining content and pedagogy in teaching and learning to teach. *Journal of Teacher Education, 51*(3), 241–247.

Barbetta, P. M., Norona, K. L., & Bicard, D. F. (2005). Classroom behavior management: A dozen common mistakes and what to do instead. *Preventing School Failure, 49*(3), 11–19.

Bloom, B. (1956). *Taxonomy of educational objectives. Handbook I: Cognitive domain.* New York: David McKay.

Bosch, K. A. (1991). Cooperative learning: Instructions and procedures to assist middle school teachers. *Middle School Journal, 22*(3), 34–35.

Bosch, K. A., & Kersey, K. (1993). Teaching problem-solving strategies. *Clearing House, 66*(4), 228–230.

Bosch, K. A., & Kersey, K. (2000). *The first-year teacher: Teaching with confidence.* Washington, DC: NEA Professional Library, National Education Association.

Bowers, C. A., & Flinders, D. J. (1990). *Responsive teaching: An ecological approach to classroom patterns of language, culture, and thought.* New York: Teachers College Press.

Boyer, E. L. (1995). *The basic school.* Princeton, NJ: The Carnegie Foundation for the Advancement of Teaching.

Brigham, F., Renfro, A. K., & Brigham, M. M. (1994). *Instruction and classroom management: A combination that is music to your ears.* (ERIC Document Reproduction Service No. ED 374 109)

Brophy, J. (1981). Teacher praise: A functional analysis. *Review of Educational Research, 51*, 5–32.

Brown, D. (2004). Urban teachers' professed classroom management strategies: Reflections of culturally responsive teaching. *Urban Education, 39*(3), 266–289.

Burke, K. (1992). *What to do with the kid who. . . .* Arlington Heights, IL: IRI/SkyLight.

Canter, L., & Canter, M. (1976). *Assertive discipline.* Santa Monica, CA: Lee Canter & Associates.

Charles, C. M. (1992). *Building classroom discipline* (4th ed.). White Plains, NY: Longman.

Charles, C. M. (1999). *Building classroom discipline* (6th ed.). Boston: Pearson Education.

Charles, C. M. (2005). *Building classroom discipline* (8th ed.). Boston: Pearson Education.

Cochran-Smith, M., & Lytle, S. (1999). The teacher research movement: A decade later. *Educational Researcher, 28*(7), 15–25.

Cruickshank, D. (1987). *Reflective teaching: The preparation of students of teaching.* Reston, VA: Association of Teacher Educators.

Edwards, C. H. (1997). *Classroom discipline and management*. Upper Saddle River, NJ: Prentice Hall.

Elam, S., Rose, L. C., & Gallup, A. M. (1997a). The 28th annual Phi Delta Kappa/Gallup Poll of the public's attitudes toward the public schools. In F. Schultz (Ed.), *Education 97/98: The annual editions series* (pp. 26–43). Guilford, CT: Dushkin/McGraw-Hill.

Elam, S., Rose, L. C., & Gallup, A. M. (1997b). The 28th annual Phi Delta Kappa/Gallup Poll of the public's attitudes toward the public schools. In F. Schultz (Ed.), *Education 98/99: The annual editions series* (pp. 27–37). Dubuque, IA: McGraw-Hill.

Elliot, J. (1991). *Action research for educational change*. Buckingham, UK: Open University Press.

Emmer, E. T., Evertson, C. M., Clements, B. S., & Worsham, M. E. (1997). *Classroom management for secondary teachers* (4th ed.). Boston: Allyn & Bacon.

Emmer, E. T., Evertson, C. M., Sanford, J. P., Clements, B. S., & Worsham, M. E. (1989). *Classroom management for secondary teachers*. Englewood Cliffs, NJ: Prentice Hall.

Emmer, E. T., Evertson, C. M., & Worsham, M. E. (2003). *Classroom management for secondary teachers* (6th ed.). Boston: Allyn & Bacon.

Enz, B. J. (1997). *Teacher's toolbox: A primer for new professionals*. Dubuque, IA: Kendall/Hunt.

Evertson, C. M. (1989). Improving elementary classroom management: A school-based training program for beginning the year. *Journal of Educational Research, 83*, 82–90.

Evertson, C. M. (1995). *Classroom organization and management program*. (Revalidation Submission to the Program Effectiveness panel). Washington, DC: U.S. Department of Education. (ERIC Document Reproduction Service No. ED 403 247)

Evertson, C. M., Emmer, E. T., Clements, B. S., Sanford, J. P., & Worsham, M. E. (1989). *Classroom management for elementary teachers*. Englewood Cliffs, NJ: Prentice Hall.

Gardner, H. (1993). *Multiple intelligences: The theory in practice*. New York: Basic Books.

Glasser, W. (1969). *Schools without failure*. New York: Harper & Row.

Glasser, W. (1986). *Control theory in the classroom*. New York: Harper& Row.

Glasser, W. (1993). *The quality school teacher*. New York: Harper Perennial.

Jones, V. F., & Jones, L. S. (1995). *Comprehensive classroom management*. Needham Heights, MA: Allyn & Bacon.

Jones, V. F., & Jones, L. S. (2004). *Comprehensive classroom management*. Boston: Pearson Education.

Kohn, A. (1996). *Beyond discipline: From compliance to community*. Alexandria, VA: Association of Supervision and Curriculum Development.

Kounin, J. (1977). *Discipline and group management in classrooms* (Rev. ed.). New York: Holt, Rinehart & Winston.

Little, J. (1990). The mentoring phenomenon and the social organization of teaching. In C. B. Cazden (Ed.), *Review of research in education, 16,* 297–351. Washington DC: American Education Research Association.

Loughran, J., & Russell, T. (Eds.). (1997). *Teaching about teaching: Purpose, passion, and pedagogy in teacher education*. London: Falmer.

Marzano, R. (2003). *What works in schools*. Alexandria, VA: Association for Supervision and Curriculum Development.

Morehead, M., & Cropp, D. (1994). Enhancing preservice observation experience with structured clinical experiences. *The Teacher Educator, 29*(4), 2–8.

Nelsen, J., Lott, L., & Glenn, J. (2000). *Positive discipline in the classroom* (rev. ed.). Rocklin, CA: Prima.

Reed, A. J. S., & Bergemann, V. E. (1995). *In the classroom* (2nd ed.). Guilford, CT: Dushkin.

Roberts, R., Kellough, R., & Moore, K. (2006). *A resource guide for elementary school teaching.* Upper Saddle River, NJ: Pearson Education.

Rogers, C., & Freiberg, H. J. (1994). *Freedom to learn.* Columbus, OH: Merrill.

Rose, L. C., & Gallup, A. M. (2005). The 36th annual Phi Delta Kappa/Gallup Poll of the public's attitudes toward the public schools. In F. Schultz (Ed.), *Education 05/06 7: The annual editions series* (pp. 17–27). Dubuque, IA: McGraw-Hill.

Rowe, M. (1974). Wait-time and rewards as instructional variables: Their influence on language, logic, and fate control. Part one: Wait-time. *Journal of Research in Science Teaching, 11,* 81–94.

Schon, D. (1983). *The reflective practitioner: How professionals think in action.* New York: Basic Books.

Simmons, B. J. (2002, Summer). Navigating the first year of teaching. *Kappa Delta Pi Record, 38*(4), 160–164.

Sylwester, R. A. (1995). *Celebration of neurons.* Alexandria, VA: Association of Supervision and Curriculum Development.

Tobin, K. (1987). The role of wait time in higher cognitive level learning. *Review of Education Research, 57,* 69–95.

Veenman, S. (1984). Perceived problems of beginning teachers. *Review of Education Research, 54,* 143–178.

Wang, M. C., Haertel, G. D., & Walberg, H. J. (1994). What helps students learn? *Educational Leadership, 51*(4), 74–79.

Wolfgang, C. H. (1995). *Solving discipline problems: Strategies for classroom teachers* (3rd ed.). Boston: Allyn & Bacon.

Wong, H., & Wong, R. (1998). *The first days of school.* Mountain View, CA: Harry Wong Publications.

Wong, L. (1990, July). *Trainees' perceptions of competence and control in teaching.* Paper presented to the International Council on Education for Teaching, Singapore.

Index

**CORWIN
PRESS**

The Corwin Press logo—a raven striding across an open book—represents the union of courage and learning. Corwin Press is committed to improving education for all learners by publishing books and other professional development resources for those serving the field of PreK–12 education. By providing practical, hands-on materials, Corwin Press continues to carry out the promise of its motto: **"Helping Educators Do Their Work Better."**